THE REAL DISASTER IS ABOVE GROUND

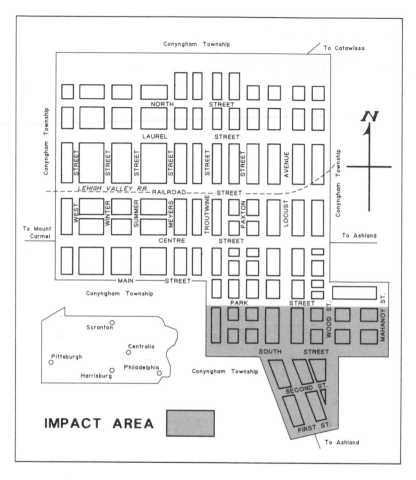

Centralia, Pennsylvania

THE REAL DISASTER IS ABOVE GROUND

A Mine Fire & Social Conflict

J. STEPHEN KROLL-SMITH
& STEPHEN ROBERT COUCH

THE UNIVERSITY PRESS OF KENTUCKY

Scholarly publisher for the Commonwealth,
serving Bellarmine College, Berea College, Centre
College of Kentucky, Eastern Kentucky University,
The Filson Club, Georgetown College, Kentucky
Historical Society, Kentucky State University,
Morehead State University, Murray State University,
Northern Kentucky University, Transylvania University,
University of Kentucky, University of Louisville,
and Western Kentucky University.

Editorial and Sales Offices: Lexington, Kentucky 40506-0336

Library of Congress Cataloging-in-Publication Data

Kroll-Smith, J. Stephen, 1947–
    The real disaster is above ground : a mine fire and social
conflict / J. Stephen Kroll-Smith and Stephen Robert Couch.
        p.   cm.
    ISBN 0-8131-1667-8 (alk. paper)
    1. Mine fires—Social aspects—Pennsylvania—Centralia.
2. Centralia (Pa.)—Social conditions.   3. Mine fires—Social
aspects—Case studies.   4. Social conflicts—Case studies.
I. Couch, Stephen Robert.
TN315.K76   1989
363.3'497—dc20   89-39905
                                                          CIP

This book is printed on acid-free paper meeting
the requirements of the American National Standard
for Permanence of Paper for Printed Library Materials.

Contents

Preface

Increasingly, the specter of technological risk is haunting modern culture. From the newly discovered sulfites in our beer and urethane in our wine to questions of too much ozone in the lungs or too little in the atmosphere, to the choice between losing equity in a house contaminated by dioxin or remaining in a condition of imminent danger, we face a kaleidoscope of technological risks. The origin of these threats and how they are distributed symbolize the relationship people have to one another and to their environment.

Many voices condemn errant technology as the source of most modern day risks. Machines, they argue, are polluting the garden. Others blame overpopulation and the increasing demand on the world's resources as the cause of technological expansion and increasing risks. Still others find the consumptive habits of modern families fueling the technological engine and its dangerous effluents. This story about a mine fire in Centralia, Pennsylvania, and the stories of dozens of other neighborhoods polluted by the products of industrial technology, suggest that the real source of modern technological risk is the relationship between technology and modes of economic production designed to produce things faster and cheaper by allocating the hazardous byproducts of production to those most defenseless against them. These modern tragedies also illustrate the inability of government to develop effective policies to prevent the growth and spread of technological hazards and to respond adequately to technological catastrophes when they do occur.

While all of the above is largely true of industrial societies, be they capitalist or socialist, the process by which technological risks are developed and dealt with differs depending on the social

modes of economic production. Marx recognized early that human health and the social fabric of communities are parts of the
environment that capitalist social relations manipulate for expansion and profit. People and their communal lives are part of
the resources that other people exploit for market purposes. It
is our belief that this book and others on towns and neighborhoods ravaged by environmental contaminants illustrate a need
to ponder anew the problem of social justice. As long as we
believe that the welfare of society is linked to monopoly capital
expansion—that a just society is based on converting the natural
environment into corporate profit and distributing the productive
wastes to the relatively powerless and less advantaged—there
will be books to write and lectures to attend about local towns
and neighborhoods contaminated by the wastes of modernity.

Whatever strengths this book possesses have required the
work and good will of many people. Several research assistants
helped us at various stages of the project. Barbara Knox Homrighaus, Susan Kroll-Smith, Ronald Andruscavage, and Michael
J. Kryjak, in particular, provided a valuable service in gathering
and coding historical and field data. Thanks also go to the Centralia high school students who helped gather survey data; to the
several undergraduates who coded survey data; and to Marianne
Pindar who supervised the coding. Three people deserve special
recognition: Jim Staudenmeier, whose faith in the project, if not
in all our reasons for requiring additional money and time, helped
to sustain the research in its critical early stages; Frank Clemente,
whose support as our department head was unflagging; and Lau-
ren McCallum, whose substantive and editorial suggestions
added appreciable to the quality of this book. We must recognize
the fine bibliographic support provided by Hazleton Campus
librarian Richard Tyce and his colleagues Kathleen Stone and
Dolores Mhley. Appreciation also goes to Rick Cannella for re-
cording parts of the Centralia story on film. The following colleagues and friends donated their insights, ideas, and criticisms
to early drafts of the manuscript: Margaret Cote, Bill Ellis, Paul

Lukehart, Joe Marchesani, Donald Miller, and Alan Price. We extend special thanks to Adeline Levine, whose close reading of an early draft provided many important insights and whose own work on the Love Canal served as a valuable guide and inspiration.

Many organizations also deserve recognition for their assistance. Chief among them is Penn State, which provided financial support through a Research Initiation Grant and several grants from the Faculty Scholarship Support Fund. The Hazleton and Schuylkill Campuses of Penn State also helped by providing us with reassigned time with which to carry out this project. We also appreciate the clerical and typing skills of many members of the university staff, especially Jane Cochran and Marie Kahler. Special thanks are also due to the Pennsylvania National Bank, which provided us with a small grant and with office space in Centralia, and to the law firm of Spiegel and McDermott, which gave us access to its nonconfidential Centralia-related records.

Kroll-Smith also wants to thank Tom Burns, a mentor and friend whose felicity with symbolic thought keeps him thinking about the deep meaning of almost everything, including this work. In addition, Kroll-Smith owes special thanks to Joe Tamney, Sam Klausner, Victor Lidz, and Diane Crane, his teachers at Ball State and the University of Pennyslvania. He also wants to recognize Sam Garula, a cherished friend whose special talents helped make this book, and Centralia's relocation, a reality. Finally, and with an appropriate shift to the first person, I owe a deep debt to Susan Kroll-Smith for reminding me that, in the end, relationships are more important than books.

Couch extends special appreciation to his mentors at Oberlin College and S. U. N. Y. Binghamton, most especially to Steve Cutler, John Flint, Terry Hopkins, Kiyoshi Ikeda, Jim Walsh, and Milt Yinger, and to a former colleague at the Smithsonian Institution, Roy Bryce-Laporte, who in very different but important ways taught him to appreciate and make sense of the depth and complexity of social life. He also wishes to thank his wife, Kathy

Couch, and his daughter Amanda Couch who, unable to be at the starting gate of this project, gave much support down the home stretch.

We dedicate this book to the few present and many former residents of Centralia.

Introduction:
A Dying Coal Town

Northern Appalachia is a region of contrasts. In some ways it is like other predominantly rural areas of the Northeast. In some ways it resembles the rest of Appalachia to the south. In others ways it is unique.

Many of the contrasts are quickly apparent to visitors who drive south from Danville, Pennsylvania, on State Route 54. Mile after mile of rich farmland stretches among rolling hills, dotted with handsome farm buildings and occasional suburban ranch houses. As the hills give way to more mountainous terrain, the farms become fewer and the rich black soil fades away into patches of gray-red dust. The skyline is dominated by mountains. On some are large black patches where vegetation once grew; others look as if their sides have been gouged out; still others end abruptly in flat tops, as if their heads have been cut off. Tall pines and stately maples and oaks give way to small white birches sticking precariously like pins out of the sides of the mountains.

After merging with Route 61 the road widens to four lanes and crosses an area formerly strip-mined for coal, now a black, desolate plain. Five miles later the highway enters the Borough of Centralia. Not long ago, well-kept single-family homes and row houses lined the street. But now, in the spring of 1985, Centralia has the appearance of a ghost town—or, more accurately, a town that is dying. Interspersed among the occupied homes are boarded-up houses, their paint peeling and their lawns unkempt.

Beyond a neat white Methodist church and a few shops, a stop sign marks the center of downtown. A couple of customers walk

into the Pennsylvania National Bank's small branch office; a few
teenagers hang out at the cycle shop. This is a small town in very
slow motion.

After Route 61 turns right at the stop sign, it climbs a hill past
more boarded-up homes and businesses. A VFW post still op-
erates in a building set back from the road but all around are
vacant lots bearing the scars of recent demolition, posted with
Keep Off signs. A small building that looks like a former church
is identified by a sign as a teen center, now abandoned. So far
there is not even a clue as to why the town is dying.

At the crest of the hill lie a handsome Roman Catholic church
and rectory, with a parochial school across the street. Just beyond
the school stands a patch of dead trees. On a clear dry day, there
is nothing more threatening to be seen. But when the temperature is cool and the air is moist, white steam pours from the
ground around the trees and blows across the road. The very
roots of the trees appear to be smoldering, but no flames are
seen—only billowing clouds of acrid steam. To the right, steam
oozes eerily from the side of a small hill. Even the rocks seem
to be blasted white from the heat beneath. At night, when the
weather is damp and chilly, a couple of low-wattage street lights
serve only to illuminate the gaseous steam that belches from the
earth. There is an almost overwhelming sense that danger is
close.

Like many anthracite coal mining communities, the Borough
of Centralia is dying. But the immediate cause of its destruction
is unique: an underground mine fire that has been burning for
a quarter of a century, like an insidious environmental demon
far below the earth's surface. Just as coal was the reason for its
birth, coal is now the agent of Centralia's death.

From the founding of the borough in 1866, life in Centralia
revolved around the mining and processing of anthracite coal.
The decline of the anthracite industry during the first half of this
century brought down the population of Centralia along with it.
By mid-century, most of the thousand or so inhabitants were
elderly and poor or working class.

The fire that is eating away at Centralia originated in 1962 in
a garbage dump on an abandoned mine stripping at the south-
eastern edge of the borough. When the initial fire-fighting efforts
failed, the blaze ignited an outcropping of coal. From there it
spread underground into the abandoned mine shafts that ho-
neycomb the ground under and around Centralia. State and federal governments spent over $5 million over the following two
decades without halting the fire's underground march.

Despite the failure to contain or extinguish it, the underground monster did little visible damage for years. But in 1969
carbon monoxide gas drove three Centralia families from their
homes. In 1976 carbon monoxide in a concentration twenty times
the lethal dose for a human being was found pouring from a
borehole twenty-seven feet from the doorstep of another Centralia home. In 1979 a service station was ordered closed because
of rising gasoline temperatures in its underground storage tanks.
The following year the federal government purchased seven borough properties considered to be unsafe; others followed. More
and more residents complained of physical illness that they attributed to the fire.

A turning point came on Valentine's Day in 1981, when a
twelve-year-old boy fell into a cave-in caused by the mine fire
and escaped death only be grasping onto an exposed tree root.

Several Centralians responded to this near-tragedy by forming
a community action group to push for an adequate governmental
response. But instead of rushing to join the new group, most
Centralia residents became hostile toward its members. Government efforts to control the fire continued to fail. Public meetings, scheduled more frequently, became occasions for residents
to express bitter hostility against the government and against
each other. This small-town community became the scene of
telephone threats, tire slashings, and a fire bombing. No fewer
than seven grassroots community organizations sprang up among
the one thousand inhabitants, each group offering a different
perspective and proposals, and each prepared to fight for its
views.

In July of 1983 a resolution of one sort was achieved when a government-sponsored engineering study judged the fire to be even worse than anyone had thought. It concluded that if left to burn itself out, the fire would make all of Centralia uninhabitable, but continued efforts to control or extinguish the blaze would also make life in Centralia intolerable. The solution: Centralia must go. In October of 1983 the U.S. Congress authorized the sum of $42 million dollars for purchase of Centralians' property. The vast majority of Centralians accepted the government's offer to buy their property, and the relocation is now under way.

But the costs of the Centralia mine fire cannot be measured merely in terms of property loss, ill health, poor financial position, or environmental degradation. Other losses are less tangible in nature but no less painful. The Centralia story is one of residents who lost faith in government and in each other. It is the story of rancorous discord as neighbor blamed neighbor for the protracted trauma that threatened to continue without end. It is the story of an ecological disaster that stripped away the facade of community to reveal a segmented, uncoordinated collective that was ill prepared to unite in the interests of the town as a whole. It is the story of municipal government, citizens' groups, and informal cliques bringing unrealistic grievances against inappropriate targets through ineffective strategies. It is the story of a village unable to invoke criteria of shared experience or communal affiliation to interpret or resolve its crisis.

This book examines a small town's response to an increasingly common type of adversity, the chronic technological disaster. We will look closely at the frantic and largely futile search within Centralia for a medium of discourse agreeable to a majority of resident for defining the scope and seriousness of a long-term, human-caused disaster that could be eased or extinguished only by technological intervention. We will show how the complicated and confusing phenomena of risk perception and threat beliefs aggravated the rancorous conflict within the town. We will also follow the path of a disaster agent that resisted the intervention of expensive, sophisticated, cutting-edge technology, posing unique problems for legislators, scientists, and, most of all, the affected community.

The Centralia story is a tale complicated by the power of technological reasoning to preclude other, arguably more appropriate, modes of defining issues. Decisions of a technological nature in fact masked political choices, while the community was too conflict-ridden to demand prompt, effective action. Ironies abound. For example, a sense of community began to emerge in Centralia only when the death of the community was assured. And when government finally took decisive action, it was to buy and demolish Centralia, not to save it.

The residents' own words lend human proportions to the trauma of the Centralia experience. Consider the interpretations that several Centralians gave to their experiences of the fire, particularly how they interpreted the rancorous response of their neighbors to the underground blaze. In their blunt and honest appraisals, the tragedy that befell the town is thrown into sharp perspective:

Centralia went from a community that was almost placid . . . to a community that's in a constant turmoil. It's divided neighborhoods. It's created groups that work against each other. It's made me cynical in lots of ways. It's made me doubt the intentions of people. All the rumors of the coal and the money and the deals and all that stuff. . . . It makes me not want to participate. I'm sick to death of it. I go through these gamuts, from really caring what happens, to not giving a damn at all.

Centralia is like someone you know who is slowly dying of cancer; I mean, every time you turn around there is another part of town that's infected. If we would just get together we could fight this cancer. But people around here are more concerned with themselves than with their neighbors. Rumors, hostileness, prejudice, backbiting . . . this town's more sick than the fire.

The fire has split up people. It has torn people apart, you know—divided us. We're divided this and that way. We are worse than a pie cut into eight pieces.

We've lived in this town for forty-six years. We had a chance to move twice, but for me this was a good place to raise my kids. Now I want out. This fire has made people mean. Anymore, I can't even walk down to pick up my mail without someone glaring at me or, worse, calling me a name; and these people were once my friends.

People hold grudges in this town. They don't forget. And I'll tell you, I no longer respect people unconditionally. Conditional respect, that's what the fire has taught me. That is what it has taught me as a parent and I will pass it on to my children.

These passages suggest that the disaster in Centralia turned it into a place of little compassion, a town where neighbors were unwilling to care for one another, where friendships could not survive—a town, in short, that experienced an ecological crisis as a profound social and personal tragedy.

The social reality we are setting out to explain is the destructive community conflict that characterized Centralia's response to a twenty-five-year-old mine fire. The literature suggests that the social response to most disasters includes the development of a "therapeutic community," in which residents band together to help each other cope with the catastrophe. In this altruistic coalescence, community ties are strengthened and mutual cooperation is increased. In Centralia, however, the community suffered from sever, debilitating conflict. Instead of aiding and cooperating with each other, neighbor struggled against neighbor, creating as much havoc aboveground as the fire created below.

As sociologists, we faced many difficult decisions about how to study a town in the throes of social and moral collapse: What methods should we employ and how much should we become involved in the community's efforts to reach a consensus on its problem? We refer the reader to appendix A for a discussion of the ethical and methodological issues we wrestled with throughout the course of this project.

We drew on data from several sources to capture the unique

sociological dimensions of Centralia's trauma: historical records; field data in the form of participant observation and in-depth interviews; a community survey; a self-reporting stress study; and such documentary accounts as government reports and newspaper articles.

As in all communities, Centralia's social structure and culture developed over time, making a knowledge of Centralia's history essential. With the aid of two research assistants, we assembled and examined historical material to piece together a picture of the economic, social, and cultural development of the borough. The material included official documents, such as tax records, deeds, and minutes of the meetings of the Borough Council and community groups; correspondence and other personal records; and secondary historical material on Centralia and the rest of the anthracite region.

We began collecting field data in the fall of 1981 and continued fieldwork throughout the project. Accompanied by a research assistant, we attended public meetings, festivities, and church services; observed community life on the street, in public buildings, and in residents' homes; and carried on informal discussions with borough residents, government officials, and representatives of private social agencies. The fieldwork intensified in March 1983, when Stephen Kroll-Smith moved into Centralia. Renting a house for eight months in an area officially called the fire's "impact zone," he was able to observe and experience daily life in a hazardous area, as well as the response of local government and citizens' groups to the mine fire.

Kroll-Smith conducted in-depth, extended interviews of thirty-four adult residents during 1982 and 1983, using snowball sampling techniques. The open-ended, taped interviews, which lasted from one to three hours, investigated the residents' perceptions of small-town life, the mine fire, and community and governmental response to it, as well as the significance of personal and collective religious faith when a community is in crisis.

The community survey was conducted during August 1982. Questionnaires, primarily in the form of closed-ended questions, were distributed door-to-door to all adult residents of the borough and collected by the survey team two days later. A total of 368 people, or 56.9 percent of Centralia's adult population at the time, returned the questionnaires. The information collected includes demographic, socioeconomic, and attitudinal data, and residents' perceptions of their community and the mine fire.

With the cooperation of two nurses and a research assistant, we conducted a resident-reporting stress study during late 1984 and early 1985. Thirty-five respondents, selected on the basis of home location within the town, were interviewed for one to two hours each. Questions attempted to discover residents' perceptions of the amount and sources of stress in their lives.

In the last segment of our research, we examined the voluminous government correspondence, memos, and technical reports on Centralia and a complete file of local newspaper articles. These data throw much light on the chronology of events in Centralia and on the response to the fire by local, state, and national governments and organizations. Our studies extended to the relationship of the press itself to community discord.

Throughout this study three fundamental assumptions guided our analysis and structured our arguments.[1]

Our first assumption is that human social life must be viewed in an ecological context, as an integral part of the ecological system. Accordingly, this study views the mine fire as an aversive agent interrupting the normal exchanges between a community and its environment, substituting a new context and shaping the social response.

We further argue that a typology of disasters can be constructed on the basis of two dimensions—the duration of the disaster and the degree of human-technological involvement in its cause or abatement. A natural disaster may be sudden (as in an earthquake) or of long duration (as in a prolonged drought), whereas a technological disaster may continue for years, like the mine fire, or strike quickly, like the disaster at Bhopal. These characteristics can help to predict the social response to the disaster.

In ordinary usage, the word "disaster" is associated with aversive agents that strike swiftly and disappear just as suddenly, leaving in their wake destruction and probable death. A tidal wave rolling over a shoreline village is a massive, unrelenting reality that is unequivocally interpreted and responded to as a disaster. With little collective doubt about what occurred and how it should be interpreted, extra-local governments and social service agencies declare the site a disaster area, in need of relief and rehabilitation. At the local level, a therapeutic community can be expected to emerge, expanding the day-to-day roles of citizens and organizations within the community to meet the immediate needs of the injured, the homeless, and the grief-stricken.

What we shall call the chronic technological disaster (or CTD) has quite different characteristics. A CTD, such as contamination by dioxin or asbestos, lasts longer and is considerably harder to detect. Related to the difficulty in detection is the difficulty in assessing the long-term consequences. With CTDs it is frequently difficult to identify the victims objectively. Moreover, the varying ways in which people experience the disaster agent can be expected to result in significant differences in their subjective assessments of its potential for harm. Since a CTD is manmade, its abatement or disposal demands sustained technological intervention. In other words, a unique pattern of psychological, social, and cultural disruption characterizes the CTD.

Our second assumption in dealing with the effects of disaster is that a community's social and cultural history shapes its ability to respond to the events and forces that challenge it. The local social, economic, and political structures are the vehicles by which collective responses flow. The local culture is the source of the conceptual, emotional, and physical resources by which a threat is defined, meanings are determined, and responses are launched.

At this level of analysis it is particularly important to understand the differences between Centralia and the prototypical small town. Founded in 1866 as a small anthracite mining village,

Centralia grew to harbor a mixed ethno-religious population while remaining predominantly working class. Life in the borough depended almost solely on the extraction, processing, and shipping of anthracite coal. The mines, collieries, and many of the area's businesses and homes were owned by absentee coal operators who dominated community decision-making. Coal profits, far from benefiting the long-term development of Centralia itself, flowed out of the borough and into capitalist ventures in major cities along the eastern seaboard. Given the unstable nature of the mining industry, Centralia's population was in a state of constant flux, as miners and their families moved into the area in great numbers during times of prosperity, only to move on when the local economy turned sour. There was little sense of community, and group attachment within Centralia was restricted to family, church, and ethnic group.

The dependent, fragmented structure of the community, tenuously adapted to a single-industry economy, was poorly prepared to adjust to the decline of coal. As with the entire region, Centralia was deprived of the economic and human capital to attract substantial new industry; the structures and cultures of a coal-based economy were ill suited to new technologies. Frozen in time, social structures and cultural norms have changed little up to the present day, long after the economy for which they were suited has vanished. At the community level, then, Centralia's collective life can be characterized as weak and overadapted; the traditional community could not serve residents as a supportive context from which to organize a collective response to the underground fire.

Our third and final assumption is that a community is not only part of an ecological system but also of a larger social system with which it interacts constantly. Small towns are always more or less affected by their relationships with the larger social entity; they are especially affected by that system, however, in times of collective crises. In the case of a chronic technological disaster, a community's response is shaped significantly by its relationship to remote centers of power and influence.

In Centralia's case, state and federal government agencies were the primary actors at the extra-local level. These agencies have three characteristics that emerged as critical to this study. First, they are remote from Centralia in terms of geography, culture, and power; with values and world views widely divergent from those of small coal towns, influential government agencies are unlikely to be sensitive to the needs and desires of small, politically weak communities. From a distance they are even more likely to be perceived by community residents as uncaring and insensitive, an irritant to the very communities they are mandated to assist.

State and federal agencies, being bureaucratic, are governed by written rules and regulations, but there are no laws or regulations, and few precedents, for dealing with chronic technological disasters. Instead, the situation calls for innovation—the second shortfall of the government agencies in Centralia. Bureaucracies, like a community itself, are least likely to innovate effectively when the situation begs for intervention but lacks any precedent.

Complicating such situations, extra-local government power is decentralized, with a multitude of agencies at various levels sharing responsibility in any given policy area. This decentralization greatly lessens governmental ability to make policies work, aside from the fact that environmental policies themselves are frequently unclear and conflicting. Given the diffusion of authority and the considerable expense of ameliorating a chronic technological disaster, agencies may be expected to differ as to where responsibility lies.

Moreover, confronted with a technological problem that admits of many competing solutions—none of them certain, all of them expensive—and faced with a hostile community, no matter how powerless, the agency response is likely to favor short-term problem management and containment rather that long-term solution. Indeed, a primary goal of the agency might be seen as minimizing political damage to the agency itself at a minimum outlay of public expenditures.

Another source of extra-local response to the Centralia mine
fire was the social service sector. Several agencies, including
Catholic Social Services, Rural American Women, and Ralph
Nader's Public Interest Research Coalition, offered tactical and
financial support to various citizens' groups within the community. A social service agency has a vested interest in defining a
problem in terms consistent with its mandate, ensuring that some
claims about the severity and scope of the mine fire crisis would
be supported, while others would be challenged. These agencies
played an important, though unwitting, role in fostering community discord while at the same time meeting the concrete
needs of many individuals and a few of the groups in Centralia.

In the next three chapters we examine Centralia's history, the
history of the mine fire and the response of government agencies to it, and the rise among residents of the town of multiple
interpretations of what was happening. Next we describe the first
grass-roots response to the fire, analyze the conflicts that developed as competing groups emerged, and describe how Centralia's fate was at last sealed. In the concluding chapter, we try
to make sociological sense of the story by comparing some key
elements of natural calamities with those of chronic technological disasters.

In the appendix, we justify our decision to focus on the impact
of citizens' groups, government intervention, and the uncertain
march of the mine fire on the community. We discuss the methodological difficulties that followed the decision to make the community, and not any particular group, our unit of analysis.
Readers with methodological interests may want to read the appendix before continuing with the story.

1. King Coal Built a Town but Not a Community

A little over a century ago, the anthracite coal mining region of Pennsylvania was embroiled in one of the more famous labor conflicts in American history. A major part in this conflict was played by the Molly Maguires, a clandestine Irish organization considered by some to be the champions of liberty and by others, anarchic terrorists.

According to local legend, the Mollies accosted the rector of St. Ignatius Roman Catholic Church in Centralia and beat him up because of his staunch opposition to them. The priest returned to the church, rang the bell to summon his congregation, and in his anger pronounced a curse on Centralia, condemning it to destruction. A century later, the town is dying—although the effectiveness of the historical curse is open to debate.

There is no question, however, that in less dramatic ways the past of a community affects its present. It is the past that shapes the patterns in which a community responds to crises, the resources available for response, and the culture that interprets crises and channels the reaction. Much as an individual reacts to crises on the basis of a personality shaped by past experiences, the community response is based on social and cultural patterns developed through decades of collective experience.

Centralians view their history in terms quite different from what we discovered about the town's past. When asked to assess the damages wrought by the mine fire and the bitter conflict that it ignited, many Centralians mourned the decline and death of a close-knit community. "Centralia," they said, "is not like it used to be."

"There was a time," mused one resident, "when people

trusted one another here. . . . This was a real town once, not one of those cities where people get mugged while their neighbors watch. We lived in Philadelphia once but moved back because it was what we wanted. Now, with this fire, we might as well be back in the city."

For many residents of Centralia, the mine fire destroyed traditional bases for communal identity and action. Another Centralian put it this way: "The young families, they may not remember [when things were different]; this thing [the fire] has been going on for over twenty years now. They may have known nothing but the fire. That's been their whole life, the fire. But I've lived in this town for seventy-two years. This fire has torn our guts out. . . . [This] used to be the friendliest town. Didn't matter what the problem was, six people would be there to lend a hand.

"I've lived in this town all my life, and I can tell by looking at you I'm old enough to be your grandfather. Things was different here before this crazy fire business. This was a good place to live. People could rely on one another, not like now. . . . People was proud to call themselves Centralians. We're a laughingstock now. When I go out of town I don't want nobody to know I'm from this crazy town."

The media, government representatives, and social service agencies served to intensify residents' perception of a once vital settlement now dying in the grip of an underground monster. Centralians were frequently exhorted by agency personnel and legislators to put aside their differences and revitalize a shared past wherein behavior was governed by common bonds rather than by individual or factional interests. The image of the "old Centralia" as a close-knit community lost to the ravages of an underground fire was nurtured by the popular media. In newspapers, television, and a documentary film, Centralians were given the opportunity to reaffirm their perception of a past, now dying, in which the crucial quality of life was the sense of common purpose in a small town.

If such personal perceptions were relatively accurate portrayals of the "old Centralia," we would have expected residents confronted with a protracted crisis to be capable of organizing effectively, of pooling their resources in a coordinated way to achieve some resolution to their predicament. But Centralians' response to the mine fire was anything but coordinated.

The apparent discrepancy between Centralians' accounts of a shared past and their rancorous discord in responding to the fire in part reflects the gap that separated the subjective construction of the community's past from what is objectively known about its evolution. Historical remembrances may tell us more about the residents' present state of mind than about what actually happened. Remembering the "old Centralia" in terms akin to the classic primary group is less a response to recorded history than it is a reaction to present scarcities.[1] It is a perception rooted not in historical experience but in the desire for collective resources not available in the present. In short, in recalling their past people in the town were engaging in the invention of tradition, more popularly called nostalgia.

An examination of Centralia's history fails to reveal an "old Centralia" where community attachment was strong. The attachment structure was constructed at the levels of family and religious and ethnic groups rather than at the community level. The groups that Centralians were encouraged to identify with, to be guided by, fell short of representing the town as a whole. There were in fact several communities in Centralia, each with an explicit recognition of its own common interests. What passed for effective and frequent communication in town occurred more within specific ethnic and religious cultures than across them. In short, Centralia is not a typical Tocquevillian village, but an anthracite mining town.

In the mid-nineteenth century it was coal that fed the expanding industrial capacity of the United States. Over 20 million tons of coal were mined in 1860.[2] As the coal industry developed, however, chronic overproduction and overinvestment sapped the industry's initial strength.[3] The independent coal operators found themselves in a difficult economic position, as did the railroads, which could not count on a steady supply of coal to transport.

In an effort to consolidate the industry, railroad companies began buying coal land to gain control of production. The greatest coal empire of the day was built by the Philadelphia and Reading Railroad, which purchased 60,000 acres of coal land in 1871 and 40,000 additional acres over the next two years.[4]

Centralia's history is tied to that of a competitor of the Philadelphia and Reading, the Lehigh Valley Railroad, which had amassed 32,000 acres of coal land by 1873. Since its charter prohibited the direct purchase of coal lands, the Lehigh Valley gained a controlling interest in several "independent" coal companies. One of the first of the companies to be taken over was also the first to operate in Centralia: the Locust Mountain Coal and Iron Company.[5] By 1870, Centralia's long history of association with the Lehigh Valley Railroad had begun.

The coal barons were not content simply to own the land: they saw it as being in their economic interest to dominate the social and political order of the region. Their drive for dominance molded the distinctive pattern along which the anthracite mining town developed.

Geology was paramount in the thinking of the coal barons as they plotted the location of human settlements in the region: quite simply, towns and mine patches were located where the coal was. The coal seams were found in three regions—the upper (or northern), middle, and lower (southern) fields. Economically and socially, two distinct regions emerged: the northern, settled originally by farmers from Connecticut and New York; and the southern, inhabited by Pennsylvania Dutch and Pennamites. The former looked to New York for capital and markets; the latter, to Philadelphia. North or south, growth was rapid. In the northern field, Carbondale's population of 50 in 1828 had grown to 2,500 by 1833, and to nearly 5,000 by 1850. To the south, Pottsville, a hamlet of a few houses and taverns in 1825, numbered more than five hundred dwellings by 1831; by 1845 it had more than 5,000 inhabitants.[6]

Dotted among such relatively large settlements were a great many small mine towns and patches. Because of the location of coal seams and the difficulties of traversing the mountainous terrain, most settlements were isolated and quite self-sufficient. Many were company towns.[7] The advent of the railroads did little to break down the provincialism that developed; rail lines were laid to haul the coal to the eastern seaboard and to bring immigrant workers to the coal fields, not to link the various areas within anthracite country. The geographic isolation made union organizing within the region difficult throughout the nineteenth century.

In its early history, Centralia was typical of most anthracite coal communities. In 1855, the first engineer and agent of the Locust Mountain Coal and Iron Company, Alexander W. Rea, built the first home in the settlement that was to become Centralia. During the next few years, streets and lots were surveyed, several collieries were built, and homes for mine workers were constructed by the company. This settlement, surrounded by several small patch communities serving various collieries, became known as Centerville. In 1862, a post office was established, necessitating a change of name, as Pennsylvania already had a community named Centerville. At the suggestion of Alexander Rea, the name became Centralia.[8]

Into the Borough of Centralia and its environs came an influx of the skilled English and Welsh miners and Irish laborers needed to work the collieries. By 1870, the population of Centralia stood at 1,342; a decade later, it approached 2,000.[9] By 1860, several collieries were operating through leases from the Locust Mountain Coal and Iron Company and the famed Girard Estate. In the early 1860s, the Centralia and Continental collieries opened, followed by several others in 1865.[10]

Although many of its first homes were company-built dwellings, Centralia evolved into a "free" town, surrounded by small company patches attached to specific collieries. As in other free towns of the region, the mining company influenced the community's social life. For example, during the last quarter of the nineteenth century the Locust Mountain Coal and Iron Company provided land for the Methodist, Episcopal, Baptist, and Roman

Catholic churches. Breaker operators financially supported Holy Trinity Episcopal Church; one of them paid for its chancel window, complete with his monogram. The company favored fraternal organizations too, donating land for the Odd Fellows' Hall, for one. Even municipal services were targets of the operating company, the Lehigh Valley Railroad, which in 1881 paid $50,000 for a controlling interest in the newly formed Locust Mountain Water Company, which served Centralia.[11]

Retail trade in Centralia was no exception to the coal company pattern, which attempted to meet every consumer need through the aptly named Mammoth Store, which opened in 1881 with departments stocked with groceries, clothing, furniture, building supplies, and agricultural products. Household maintenance and repairs were offered, and for the farmers, "even bull service was provided."[12] In this true company store, purchases by company employees (who made up the bulk of the customers) were handled by a credit system that deducted purchases from wages.

Throughout the region, the companies made their political influence felt at all levels of government, using lobbying and patronage to the fullest. Since elected officials at the local level often sided with the miners against the operators, the companies worked to reduce the power of local officials to next to nothing.[13] Clifton Yearley points out that the Commonwealth of Pennsylvania had the legal power to control the Reading Company's voracious expansion, but did not do so because the Reading in fact constituted Pennsylvania's "interim government."[14] Perhaps the most blatant appropriation of state sovereignty by the companies occurred in the 1870s, when several reputed members of the secret Molly Maguire organization were hanged, after private detectives hired by the Reading investigated the case, company police arrested the alleged offenders, and Franklin B. Gowen, president of the Reading and a lawyer, prosecuted the case himself. As Aurand quips, "the State provided only the courtroom and hangman."[15]

The Molly Maguires, or their reputation, tore Centralia apart. Violence blamed on this clandestine society resulted in at least

four murders, including that of the town's founder, Alexander
Rea, in 1868. Many of the town's "leading citizens" fled the rash
of violence and arson.[16] Among the many breaker fires, the Centralia colliery burned three times between 1866 and 1879.[17] Nor
was the destruction directed only at the coal operators. Many
homes and businesses were torched, including an 1872 blaze that
consumed two square blocks of the town.[18] The violence, which
had class and ethnic overtones, was directed largely against coal
company agents and facilities. But it also split the Irish laboring
community itself. Some supported the Mollies, but a great many
of the Irish detested such violent tactics. Neighbor was pitted
against neighbor and son against father in a pattern of suspicion
and mistrust that would reemerge with another fire in Centralia.

Even before the time of the Molly Maguires, labor unrest
plagued the companies, in the form of a boatmen's strike on the
Schuylkill Canal in 1835,[19] and a strike by anthracite miners in
Schuylkill County in 1842—their first—which the militia was
called out to disperse.[20] The first miners' union appeared in
Schuylkill County in 1848.[21] Violent mine and railroad strikes
occurred in 1869, 1871, 1877, 1897, 1900, and 1902.[22] Centralia
workers participated in many of these strikes, as well as some
local strikes of their own.[23]

The coal companies' reaction was to pressure the government
to allow the formation of a quasi-public police force unique in
this nation's history: Pennsylvania's "coal and iron police," which
existed from 1866 to as late as 1935. Created by an act of the
Pennsylvania legislature, they were controlled and paid by the
coal and iron companies, yet were commissioned by the governor
and given the full powers of police. The dominant police in the
anthracite region during the last quarter of the nineteenth century, this force embodies the overwhelming dominance of the
coal companies over the lives of the area's inhabitants.[24]

During times of labor unrest, many coal and iron police were
commissioned to patrol company property, protect strike-break-
ers, and intimidate strikers. Violence was common. But even in
times of labor peace, the coal and iron police were the dominant

constabulary of the region. In company towns and patches, they functioned as eviction officers, debt collectors, and agents of various social services, such as public health and sanitation. In "free" towns, where they supplemented the inadequate municipal police forces, they ultimately gained the upper hand, reducing many local constabularies to figureheads.

Through these law enforcement armies, then, the companies were even able to define the boundaries of permissible behavior and to punish offenders. In Centralia what passed for legal violations and punishment of the rule breakers was dictated by authorities remote from the community, thus denying residents access to a major source of civic consciousness.[25] The overall conditions throughout the region, especially in company towns, have been compared to those in medieval fiefs.[26] A colonial analogy is in fact more apt: the anthracite regions became internal colonies to core areas along the East Coast.[27] Economic and social development was accomplished not for the sake of the coal region, but for cities along the eastern seaboard. Coal and profits flowed out of the region, helping to develop core cities, civic institutions, and the urban upper class. E. Digby Baltzell states, "If Proper Philadelphia can be said to be the capital of an empire, then its chief colony is the anthracite . . . region of northeastern Pennsylvania."[28] Conversely, the anthracite region was deprived of an indigenous upper class and, indeed, of a strong local middle class, with the most influential members of the latter being agents of the coal companies.

Although a few major companies came to dominate the life of the region, the coal giants were unable to stabilize the local economy. Fluctuations in the demand for coal created a boom-or-bust economy and frontier-like social conditions. Coal towns would expand quickly when coal production peaked, only to lose much of their population when production slacked off—an unstable pattern that inhibited the development of community attachments.

Centralia was on this roller coaster. After the violence of the 1860s and 1870s had diminished, Centralia entered into the decade of its most sustained growth and prosperity. The population of the borough rose by over 30 percent in the 1880s, to 2,761 people in 1890. In 1882, the seven Centralia-area collieries produced a combined total of 510,000 tons of coal. Local religious and labor groups showed signs of growth like the coal industry's— a bigger Methodist church building, a new Baptist congregation, additions of a school, convent, and meeting hall at the Roman Catholic church. By 1885, two labor organizations boasted a combined membership of 415 men.[29]

Centralia's period of growth, however, was to be cut short by the end of the century by a cutback in coal output. In an apparent attempt to rationalize production in the area, the Lehigh Valley acquired direct control of seven area collieries in 1896,[30] and immediately retrenched, reducing production drastically. The seven collieries, which had a combined output of more than 706,000 tons in 1890, were producing a mere 236,000 tons nine years later. Centralia suffered accordingly. While the population of the rest of Conyngham Township rose from 2,739 in 1890 to 3,037 in 1900, Centralia lost a quarter of its population, which fell from 2,761 to 2,048 during the same period.[31]

Such instability and upheaval ruled out strong community attachments and institutions. As Bertoff states, "Community ties were weak, even within towns and villages. . . . The population of most mining towns was too mobile, too transient, too quickly gathered and easily scattered again."[32]

Instead of developing a strong sense of community, Centralians and others throughout the region found social attachments at other levels. By far the most binding ties were developed at the level of the family. In the words of John E. Bodnar: "The families of this mining region . . . adhered to a persistent pattern of sharing and cooperation which was rigorously enforced. Parents provided discipline and jobs; children supplemented family income and provided care for elderly parents."[33] In the face of governmental indifference and the weighty economic and social burdens of the times, the family especially the extended family—was the major source of emotional and social security.[34]

Ethnicity and religion also provided sectors for in-group identification and out-group division. The English, Welsh, and Ger-
man Protestants who were the early settlers of the coal mining
region were joined in the middle of the nineteenth century by
large numbers of Irish Catholic mine laborers who made relatively fast progress into the more skilled miners' positions.[35] During the last quarter of the nineteenth and the first quarter of the
twentieth century, thousands of Eastern and Southern European
Catholics migrated into the region and began their advance from
the bottom of the economic pyramid. In this "new immigration,"
the number of Eastern Europeans who joined the primarily Irish
laboring population of Centralia was great enough to support the
establishment of a Greek Catholic congregation in 1910 and a
Russian Orthodox parish in 1916.[36]

In the wake of the immigrant waves, ethnicity and social class
overlapped to a large degree, as did residence patterns. In Centralia, as in the anthracite region as a whole, ethnic, religious,
and residence patterns have proved enduring, carrying over even
to the present day. They still provide lines along which, for
example, political behavior may cleave.[37]

With communal attachments limited to the family and ethno-
religious affiliations, it would have been difficult for any single
individual or group in Centralia to outline a course of community
action and persuade others in town to embark upon it. Any such
attempts at leadership would likely be rejected as arising out of
self-interest rather than representing the community as a whole.
The historical tendency to refuse a bid for leadership from within
would help undo Centralia's efforts to manage its twentieth-cen-
tury mine fire.

One of the elements of communal instability in the anthracite
region was the high incidence of physical calamities. Wallace
found that "crushes, gas explosions, underground mine fires, and
flooding [to put out the fires] repeatedly put many collieries out
of business for weeks, months, or even years at a time."[38]

Centralia did not escape the recurrent physical catastrophes.
The borough's first school, erected in 1858, was engulfed by a

mine cave-in a decade later. A replacement was destroyed by fire in 1935, along with all its records. Among the frequent breaker fires, the Centralia colliery alone burned down four times between 1866 and 1961. Between 1908 and 1912, three surface fires devastated Centralia's downtown section, and cave-ins regularly ate away at buildings and roads.[39]

Along with others throughout the anthracite region, Centralians grew to accept mining disasters as part of their way of life. As Bertoff notes, "death in the mines was an everyday matter."[40] Of course, this did nothing to blunt the pain at the death or injury of a loved one. But because coal mining carried with it the seeming inevitability of personal and environmental catastrophes, those who lived with coal miners of necessity learned to cope with what they could not change. From this point of view it is not surprising that many Centralians, as well as others of the anthracite region, believed that too much was being made of the mine fire. For many of the more elderly residents, it seemed like just another problem of the region, one which should be borne without so much fuss.

During the nineteenth century, Centralia developed as a typical small anthracite mining community, dominated by huge absentee corporations, populated by a shifting, largely immigrant working-class population, and buffeted by recurrent economic and social crises. The history of the anthracite region in the twentieth century has been shaped by the fall of "King Coal." Changes in technology that opened the door to the less labor-intensive surface, or strip, mining shared in the blame. But overshadowing all else was the precipitous decline in demand for coal, which was replaced by oil and gas as home heating fuels and by diesel and electric engines for power generation.[41] These shifts ushered in the Great Depression early for the anthracite region.

Hard times had shut down all of the Lehigh Valley's collieries by 1930, and shortly thereafter, Centralia's Mammoth Store closed and was razed.[42] Various companies attempted to continue operating during the 1930s, but with little success. In the words

of one Centralian: "There was no work at all. . . . It was bootlegging coal, picking huckleberries—I think that's what kept this
town going because we had no other source. There was no relief
at that time outside of the poor order, which was ten dollars a
month. And it wasn't easy getting that, either." By "bootlegging"
coal from small illegal mine shafts sunk on company property,
Centralians at least managed to keep warm during the long winter
months, and some of them sold the coal for a small profit. Bootlegging was so widespread that even the company police who
patrolled the coal lands were defeated. According to one infor-
mant, and in keeping with Centralians' main attachment structure, the bootleg holes were extended family operations that did
not include neighbors or friends.

The industry stabilized briefly during World War II, but the
1950s almost put an end to anthracite mining, as figures from
Schuylkill County clearly show. In 1945, the county's anthracite production was 16,731,000 tons and the industry employed
19,000 workers, but by 1960, production had fallen to 6,933,000
tons, and the workforce had declined to 6,900. Eight years later,
only 4,297,000 tons were mined in the county, employing a mere
2,646.[43] Anthracite production throughout the United States,
which stood at 19 million tons in 1960, fell to 6 million tons in
1976.[44]

Given the nature of the area's one-industry economy, it lacked
the resources to attract substantial new business. The garment
industry picked up some of the slack,[45] but by 1980 it also was
running out of steam. Waves of out-migration and chronic un-
employment hit both the region's urban centers and its smaller
communities. Centralia's population dropped steadily, from
2,449 in 1940, to 1,986 in 1950 and 1,435 in 1960.[46] It became
increasingly clear that Centralia, like so many other towns in
anthracite country, was a dying community, where social events
and celebrations became ever fewer, and even the practices of
neighboring changed as people withdrew into themselves. As
one Centralian described the changes from times past: "The older
ones would sit on the front porch. There were some Irish people,

they'd sit on the porch, smoke their pipe, and talk Irish. That's how they spend their time. You don't see much of that today."

More and more of those who stayed had to commute out of the region to find work. A high proportion of the population was elderly. Counting those who were retired, disabled (especially with coal-related injuries and diseases such as "black lung"), unemployed, or working for the public sector, many had become dependent on government services in one way or another. Once again, the communities of the anthracite region were unable to free themselves from overriding dependence on forces seen as "outside" or "alien."

While the centers of power over the region have shifted from the coal companies to big government, the area has resisted many cultural changes that have characterized more urban regions. Centralians' values remain tied to home and church and, to a certain degree, ethnic group. The descendents of independent-minded immigrants, Centralians have been dominated by outside forces and unable to develop strong social ties at the community level. When confronted by a long-term, community-wide crisis requiring a united response, the familial, religious, and ethnic attachments have ironically proved divisive for the community as a whole—a sign of weakness, not strength. It is within this context that the birth, uneven growth, and eventual death of Centralia must be viewed.

Portending the difficulties Centralia would experience in managing its responses to the underground mine fire was the town's reaction to a surface fire that occurred after the turn of the century. The patterns of response to the 1908 fire are almost uncanny in foreshadowing what would occur over half a century later.

Called "the most destructive fire in the history of the anthracite coal fields,"[47] the 1908 blaze began in an unoccupied store-room at two in the morning on Friday, December 3. Fire companies from Centralia and nearby towns responded quickly, but were hampered severely by a water shortage. As is characteristic in immediate-impact disasters, townspeople themselves pitched in, forming bucket brigades and nailing wet rugs to the building

facades to try to contain the fire. After four hours of intense
activity, sunrise revealed blackened ruins, streets filled with sal-
vaged furniture and personal possessions, and only a few walls,
posts, and chimneys left of the buildings that had occupied an
entire block. Damage was estimated at between $50,000 and
$100,000, 170 people were homeless, and fifteen businesses had
been destroyed.[48]

That evening in 1908, townspeople met at the borough hall
to form a relief committee, headed by T.W. Riley, proprietor of
the company store and soon to be president of Centralia's first
bank. Under the committee's auspices, appeals went to nearby
communities for clothing and financial aid. But the lion's share
of the work of the Centralia Relief Committee was in fact done
by the committee's Ladies' Auxiliary, led by Mrs. J.M. Hum-
phrey, wife of the superintendent of the Lehigh Valley's Centralia
collieries.[49] It was not at all unusual at the turn of the century
for the coal companies to spearhead philanthropic projects within
the coal communities, nor for the wives of company officials to
do the actual work.

The Ladies' Auxiliary not only distributed the goods collected
by the Relief Committee but was also put in charge of disbursing
the money donated, which it did as conservatively as possible.
By January 8, 1909, more than a month after the blaze, $9,200
had been collected but only $1,200 had been distributed, al-
though on January 8, it is recorded, "there are still some of the
poorer people, who lost their all in the fire, who are badly in
need of aid."[50] Besides being inadequate, these philanthropic
relief efforts precluded organization and decision-making by local
residents, including the victims.

There is no evidence that the Lehigh Valley Coal Company
provided any direct aid to the victims. As a matter of fact, the
fire exacerbated a longstanding controversy between borough
residents and the company. The problem had begun a few years
earlier when the company finished mining the deep coal veins
under the center of town and as the last step "robbed the pillars"—that is, removed the coal from the underground arches

that had been left to support the surface land. When the underground supports are removed, the result is surface subsidence, or cave-ins. Indeed, it was reported that the block that burned in 1908 was part of an area "which has been slowly sinking for the past five years," and that it had gone down over three feet in the preceding year and a half.[51]

Not satisfied with robbing the pillars, the company was determined to extract the remaining coal near the surface, at an even greater risk of subsidence. Some concerned property owners went to court to stop the company's plans, but amidst speculation that it paid lawyers on both sides, the company won. However, perhaps fearing less civilized opposition by the residents, officials held off on the mining operations.[52]

The standoff ended in the fire of 1908, which destroyed the surface dwelling above the Lehigh Valley's coal. The company seized this stroke of good fortune by offering to lease the land from each property owner for one year, during which time the coal would be mined. The workings would then be filled and "the surface made safer than at present." The company offered $300 to lease each property on "the main street," and $150 for land on "the back street."[53]

In a way uncannily similar to what a mine fire would bring about decades later, the surface fire of 1908 divided friends and neighbors over the future of the community of Centralia. The coal company had no reason to request a collective decision by property owners, nor did the owners seize the initiative and reach such a decision on their own. Instead, owner by owner, they arrived at individual decisions. Some Centralians accepted the company's offer, while others began to rebuild on the land. Newspapers have no record of public meetings on the subject, nor of committees or groups being formed. According to the minutes of the Centralia Borough Council for the period, the issue was never raised in that forum. It would seem that company power extended so far as to preclude even the rebuilding of an entire city block as a collective issue. The ability of powerful outside forces to define critical issues in their own terms has long blunted efforts by Centralians to achieve (or even develop) collective goals, even to the present day.

By January 8, 1909, little more than a month after the company made the leasing offer, at least three businesses had already contracted to rebuild on their land. Others had accepted the Lehigh Valley's terms,[54] and the company wasted no time in resuming mining operations under the borough.

The result of mining the veins close to the surface was what many Centralians had feared. On March 2, "huge fissures and cave-ins . . . appeared within 25 feet of the new structures" and the "complete extinction" of "the new Centralia" was threatened. Many property owners were irate, viewing the mining as an attempt by the company to force them to sell their land. In the same spirit exhibited by many Centralians seven decades later, the record shows that in 1909 "they refuse to be scared away, and are defying the company to drive them from their homes."[55] The conflict festered until March 30, when company officials, perhaps fearing that they would not fare as well in another court appearance, decided to halt mining under the borough. The property owners may be said to have won—but only at the price of destructive conflict.

This pattern of mistrust and uncoordinated response would repeat itself seventy years later, when Centralians again perceived themselves to be at risk from forces both inside and outside their community. Given its history, Centralia was ill-prepared to confront a long-term environmental crisis in an effective, unified manner. Accustomed to dividing along familial, ethnic, or religious lines, lacking economic power and deprived of a tradition of indigenous leadership and collective decision-making, Centralia was almost entirely lacking in the social resources to confront not only a tenacious mine fire but also giant governmental bureaucracies, which had their own interests to pursue. Centralia's past only reinforced the insidious way in which the underground fire ate away at the community itself. With the discovery of the mine fire in 1962, the final chapter of Centralia's history had begun.

2. The Engineering Puzzle, 1962-1981

A mine fire is a disaster of a very different sort from an earthquake, a tornado, or a tsunami. After a tsunami, or tidal wave, hits a shoreline, it recedes. The aftermath is frequently devastating, but survivors and relief workers can proceed to rebuild without first trying to control the disaster agent itself. It may be possible to predict a tsunami, but nobody is expected to stop it. On the other hand, the Centralia mine fire, like the dioxin contamination of Times Beach, Missouri, was of human origin, and only human technical intervention could halt its hazardous course.

In the case of a mine fire, which advances slowly but steadily through coal seams, the first and foremost problem in emergency response is to halt its progress. The official response, in other words, is less concerned about community relief and rehabilitation than about bringing the fire under control. Since advanced technological methods, high in cost, are called for in dealing with a manmade disaster agent, there is an exceptional reliance on state and federal government agencies to provide assistance.[1]

Moreover, because the immediate concern is controllability, the government tends to define chronic technological disasters as engineering puzzles rather than as human or social problems, and to assign to technical agencies the lead role in managing the crisis. The engineers and other specialists who staff such agencies are used to tackling technological, not human, problems. Because mining engineers and geologists are likely to focus on the aspects of an emergency that call for the skills and authority they possess, the personal, social, and economic dimensions of the crisis are likely to be underestimated.

So it was in the case of Centralia, which was never officially declared a disaster area. Although the community may have been at a collective loss to define its crisis, there was a consensus among state and federal officials that the fire was an engineering riddle, not a disaster, and should be managed by technical, rather than social service, agencies. In the end, a technical solution eluded the specialists, and the official information regarding the presence, extent, and severity of the invincible fire was so vague or contradictory that it did not disallow any of the competing definitions of the crisis that circulated among residents.

For nineteen years after the discovery of the Centralia mine fire, local, state, and federal governments attacked the problem of controlling the blaze. Their efforts, however costly, ended only in frustration. Time and again, a solution to the problem would be proposed and debated, contracts would be bid and awarded, and the work would be completed, but the fire burned on.

When refuse was discovered burning in an illegal garbage dump southeast of the borough limits, near the Odd Fellows Cemetery, in May 1962, borough workmen flooded the fire with water and installed a clay seal to contain it. But by July the fire had spread to a nearby outcrop of coal in the Buck Mountain vein. Since control was clearly beyond the means of the Borough of Centralia, it appealed for help to the Pennsylvania Department of Mines and Mineral Industries.[2]

In 1962, the Department of Mines notified the U.S. Bureau of Mines of the problem, and local, state, and federal officials were soon meeting with coal company representatives to discuss what to do. To cut short the fast-spreading fire, they decided to excavate the burning material. Because federal funding was un-likely without a three-month wait, the Commonwealth of Penn-sylvania decided to assume the cost of the project. To speed things along, the state designated the fire an emergency and suspended the usual bidding procedures for the project, which was budgeted at $30,000. State agencies awarded the contract to Bridy, Inc., of Atlas, Pennsylvania.[3]

Meanwhile, fire gases were spreading into active mine shafts around Centralia. On August 15, when the state ordered twenty-three mines closed because of the gases, mining ended in the Centralia area, costing 140 miners their jobs.[4]

Excavation of the fire sector began on August 23. Two months later, borehole temperatures showed that the fire had advanced beyond the area being excavated. The project was discontinued as futile, after removing 53,580 cubic yards of material and spending $27,658, all to no avail.

In November, K & H Excavating Company of Mt. Carmel, Pennsylvania, began work under a new state contract that called for drilling 80 boreholes around the fire and extinguishing it by flushing down 10,000 cubic yards of fine breaker refuse, which is noncombustible material separated from usable coal during processing. In March of 1963, the $42,420 project ended when the money ran out. As of May 1963, one year after the fire had been discovered and after $70,000 had been spent to control it, it still burned on and its surface effects could be seen 700 feet from its origin.

At this point, the state was stymied, since it could not afford the $160,000 for a combination of flushing and trenching that looked like the best bet.[5] In July, the state awarded Bridy, Inc., a more limited contract of $36,225 to dig a trench to limit the fire's eastward advance, but in October, fire was discovered on both sides of the incomplete trench. The total by then: $106,000, which had achieved no degree whatsoever of fire control.[6]

Frustrated in its piecemeal attempts to battle the blaze with severely limited funds, the state made no new moves to curtail the fire for a year and a half. But in 1965, a new source of funding, this time of major proportions, became available. In March of that year, the 89th U.S. Congress passed the Appalachian Redevelopment Act, designed "to provide public works and economic development programs and the planning and coordination needed to assist in development of the Appalachian Region." The law gave the Secretary of the Interior authority over projects that rehabilitated land damaged by previous mining practices, including the extinguishing of mine fires.

In June of 1965, the Commonwealth of Pennsylvania and the U.S. Bureau of Mines submitted a joint proposal to the Appalachian Regional Commission to stop the fire once and for all. The first phase of the project, at a cost of $300,000 would attempt to cut off the air flow to the fire and to discover its exact location. The second phase would dig an isolation trench to contain the fire permanently. The projected cost of phase two: $2.2 million.[7]

The Appalachian Regional Commission approved the project and agreed to pay 75 percent of the cost, the maximum allowable under the law.[8] The state would pay most of the remainder. Under the contract for phase one, Empire Contracting Company of Old Forge, Pennsylvania,[9] completed work on November 30, 1967, at a cost of $326,123.

Early the following year, however, when the U.S. Bureau of Mines analyzed the data collected during phase one, the results indicated that phase two would cost $4.5 million, or twice the original estimate. Phase two was scrapped, and the U.S. Bureau of Mines decided instead to construct barriers of noncombustible fly ash, at the cost of a mere $519,000.[10] In April 1969, the contract was awarded to Stearns Service Company of Wilkes-Barre, which began work early the following month.

At this point, when the fire had been burning unchecked for seven years, families near it were becoming fearful about the possible health effects of gases from the blaze; some complained of frequent headaches.[11] On May 22, three families were evacuated from their homes at Wood and South Streets after a state mine inspector found trace readings of carbon monoxide in the basement of one of the dwellings.[12] The health risks of the fire appeared to be officially confirmed.

The warnings, though subtle, mounted. One family in the impact zone found its pet canary dead and concluded, since canaries are very sensitive to carbon monoxide, that gases from the fire had killed their pet. Others who lived near the fire reported difficulty in breathing. After investigating the conditions at one home, a state mine inspector stated: "I would not sleep in that house if it were mine." But the inspector had no authority to order families to leave their dwellings. Indeed, confusion reigned as to who, if anyone, had the authority to help people driven from their homes by the fire.[13]

The lack of any precedent for coping is a general problem in chronic technological disasters. Complicating the issue, authority for response to environmental problems in general is decentralized in the United States, located in a myriad of agencies at many levels of government. There is likely to be an appearance, at least, of buck-passing, and confusion in the affected community about who is in charge of what.

Disenchanted with governmental efforts, residents of Centralia criticized the fly ash project that had just begun in the spring of 1969. Fearing that the technology would not be adequate, some demanded that a trench be dug to protect them and their homes.[14] Indeed, the fly ash barrier was considered no more than a demonstration project at the time,[15] and not a few residents were incensed at the use of an experimental technology when their health—perhaps their lives—seemed to be at stake.

Elected officials responded to their concerns.[16] In June, the U.S. Bureau of Mines approved an emergency change in the contract that would allow excavation to take place, in addition to the fly ash barrier, to eliminate the fumes in homes near the fire. Adding about $100,000 to the cost of the project,[17] some 12,000 tons of coal were dug out,[18] and in August of 1970, the entire project was completed. Total cost: $582,693.

But the coal below ground was still smoldering. When borehole data indicated that the fire had crossed an anticline in the southeast portion of the impact zone, yet another contract was awarded. The Stearns Company was to construct an eastern barrier, at a projected cost of $1,352,125[19] a project that took over three years to complete.

Meanwhile, the U.S. Bureau of Mines in 1971 sponsored an excavation to the east of Locust Avenue, the main north-south street in the borough. Burning coal—the fire itself—was encountered 500 to 800 feet east of Locust Avenue. The Bureau of Mines then asked Columbia County to contribute half the cost of completing the excavation, but the county could not come up with the requested $25,000. Digging then ceased and the excavation was backfilled, leaving the coal to burn.[20] Many believe that for lack of $50,000, a comparatively small sum, the authorities lost the chance to stop the fire for good.

In government agency response to the Centralia mine fire from 1962 to 1971, controllability became a political issue. Given the technical uncertainties and the policy vacuum in the area of chronic technological disasters, engineering projects became subject to legislative debate and political intrigues. For more than a few people, both in and out of town, the first decade of government's management of the crisis left little doubt that technical decisions only imperfectly masked political choices.

In December of 1973, when the eastern fly ash barrier project was completed, at a cost of a whopping $1.8 million, there was hope that the fire had been defeated. Over the seven years of the joint federal-state venture, 1635 boreholes had been dug, 122,556 tons of fly ash injected, 117,220 cubic yards of sand flushed, 60,000 cubic yards of material excavated, 19,000 cubic yards of clay seals installed; and $2,768,208 spent. The solution appeared to hold for two and a half years. But in August of 1976, the Bureau of Mines determined that more money was needed to reinforce the existing fly ash barriers, and the following month the state Department of Environmental Resources requested funds from the Appalachian Regional Commission.[21] The proposal to reinforce the existing barriers called first for drilling boreholes to determine the extent of the problem and then for flushing, to reinforce the existing barrier or create new ones.[22] In the spring of 1977, $385,000 was approved for the project. What followed was a bureaucratic nightmare of endless delays that thwarted fire control efforts.

Although the project won funding in the spring, the cooperative funding agreement was disputed by the federal Bureau of Mines and the state Department of Environmental Resources, holding up the contract award. In September, the problem was resolved, and the contract went to the L.R. Costanzo Company of Scranton. But since the low bid of $429,550 exceeded the approved funding, the flushing project was put on hold while additional money was sought from the federal, state and county governments. Finally, in January of 1978, the funding was approved and the contract awarded. Work began on February 1.[23]

Even as far back as the planning stage for reinforcing the barriers, however, many Centralians were convinced that the fire had moved past those barriers.[24] In December 1976, state inspectors had reported evidence that poisonous gases were venting near Centralians' homes. By the time the flushing project was completed in November of 1978, at a higher than anticipated cost of $498,138, the Bureau of Mines had realized that yet more work was needed. The latest strategy returned to a previous approach: isolate the fire by digging a trench.

Seven homes in Centralia stood in the path of the proposed excavation, and the Bureau of Mines designated twenty-one other properties with homes to provide a "safety zone." The plan to acquire the homes generated heated controversy. The Bureau of Mines lacked authority to purchase the homes, but the plan was presented to the Centralia Borough Council, which gave its approval at a public meeting attended by perhaps 500 citizens. After the Bureau of Mines approved the plans, the Appalachian Regional Commission committed some funds. But as the plans continued to develop, cost estimates skyrocketed to $10 million, much of it to come from state and local sources. At this point, the state and county withdrew, the trenching project was dropped, and no other options were put on the table. Naturally, Centralians' confidence in the Bureau of Mines was further undermined. Why couldn't the bureau make up its mind?[25]

Apparently, changes within the federal bureaucracy were behind the lack of alternative plans during 1978-79. In August 1977, Congress passed the Surface Mining and Reclamation Act, which provided "for the cooperation between the Secretary of the Interior and the States with respect to the regulation of surface coal mining operations, and the acquisition and reclamation of abandoned mines, and for other purposes." The legislation set up the Office of Surface Mining and Reclamation (OSM), which would reclaim abandoned coal mine lands with funding mandated from active mines. The OSM was authorized to purchase private land as part of its reclamation efforts.[26]

Although the Office of Surface Mining was good news for Centralia in that it represented a new source of funding to combat the mine fire, there were inevitable delays while the OSM geared up. For a time, it seems, the Bureau of Mines was in a holding pattern, waiting for an initiative from the OSM. Once the OSM took an active role in Centralia, it became a new source of confusion.

During 1979, the Bureau of Mines and state officials developed a cheaper alternative to the abandoned trench idea. Slated to cost $6 million, the plan called for filling a 35-acre tract of land with fly ash slurry and other noncombustible material and sealing it in place with cement grouting. To be completed in four or five years, the project, like others before it, was touted as a final solution to the problem. Bureau of Mines experts believed the plan would work, but OSM experts disagreed. A memo to the director of the OSM from the director of the OSM's Region 1, which includes the anthracite fields of northeastern Pennsylvania, states that "the proposed project would neither extinguish nor confine the fire." Indeed, it was argued, previous "boreholes have increased the air circulation in the underground fire area," thereby feeding the fire. (The memo also notes a difficulty in obtaining information from the Bureau of Mines.)

The summary of Region 1's position even betrays a concern that the fire may be beyond control: "Until adequate analytical information is made available, and pending appropriate analysis, no further drilling should be undertaken. The technology for extinguishing the fire may not be available. Extinguishing the fire by known techniques could be impossible and at the very least prohibitively expensive. After we have reviewed all the document which we need from the Bureau of Mines we may recommend a minimal program of sealing entries and other sources of air which feed the fire."[27]

This memo, which was to have been "administratively restricted," nevertheless became public in August 1979,[28] and Centralians were both shaken and incensed by its contents. Many doubted the sincerity of the OSM's previously expressed intention to put an end to the mine fire. Other seized on the apparent lack of dialogue between the Bureau of Mines and the OSM, charging that Centralia was caught in the middle of a bureaucratic power struggle between the two agencies. Most agreed that too little was being done.[29] Finally, at the end of December, some progress appeared to be made when the Bureau of Mines and the OSM entered into an agreement under which the OSM would provide the bureau with $137,400 to drill boreholes, map the status of the fire, and develop alternative strategies for final abatement.[30]

Month by month, the fire below was growing more threatening. On December 8, 1979, rising temperatures near underground gasoline storage tanks caused the closing of a service station.[31] Early in 1980, the OSM declared an emergency in removing several families on East Park Street because of rising subsurface temperatures. Nearly $70,000 was spent on flushing to protect the St. Ignatius Elementary School[32] and nearby residences from spreading gases.

In January of 1980, an OSM document stated: "The potential for carbon monoxide and other gases seeping into homes above the fire area is an extreme danger to the public health and safety,"[33] specifically on eight properties where the OSM proposed relocations. In April, it began making offers to acquire these properties, and by the end of June, all but one family had accepted the proposed relocation.[34]

The "extreme danger" was not limited to these eight homes. In January and again in March, OSM officials had been alerted to rising CO_2 levels in the basements of two homes on South Locust Street. In late April, frustrated by the lack of government response, the owner of one of the residences called OSM officials in Wilkes-Barre and in West Virginia, alarmed because his daughter had been hospitalized with respiratory problems, and her physician recommended that she not return to her home because of its oxygen deficiency. He was told that nothing could be done. When the concerned father persisted by calling the OSM office in Washington, he finally got action. The OSM declared an emergency and authorized $50,000 for drilling and flushing under both the homes on South Locust, as well as a third.[35] Acquisition of the properties eventually became a consideration.

But the lack of clear legislative authority concerning chronic technological disasters continued to make itself felt. A memo from an OSM official concerning the acquisition of the original eight properties expressed concern about the wording used by another OSM official, specifically "OSM's PA Department's use of words 'potentially dangerous area.' The words are inflammatory, provocative and designed to give rise to fear. If this is a dangerous area, and if this is the only criteria for acquisition then everyone in the fire area can sue us and ask that OSM acquire their homes."[36]

By the fall of 1980, it became apparent that the emergency flushing activities had not protected the three Locust Street residences from dangerous gases. At a public meeting in Centralia on September 29-30, according to an OSM memo, OSM officials "did state conclusively that as a part of the overall plan at Centralia, upon a finding by the Pennsylvania Department of Health that a given residence was no longer suitable for human habitation due to levels of toxic gases from the mine fire, OSM would immediately relocate or dislocate residents to temporary quarters until some permanent remedial action could be taken. Failing any successful remedial action, the affected residence would then be acquired or moved." One of the affected residents was granted OSM permission to move to a temporary residence.[37]

When the OSM legal office became aware of this action, however, it raised objections. In an October 31 memo, a Region 1 field solicitor stated: "We are of the opinion that Title IV [of Public Law 95-87] does not envision or authorize such relocation expenses unless the property in question must be taken or vacated as an actual integral part of the reclamation and/or abatement process. The fact that the dwellings may have been declared uninhabitable would not in itself give us the authority to purchase the property or pick up the relocation expenses of the occupants."[38]

Frustration at the impasse was clearly expressed by OSM's Region 1 director: "We are faced with a very serious dilemma. Based on the authority which was passed on to us verbally . . . we did, in fact, make several statements in Centralia which charted our course of action. . . . Now there is a very serious question as to whether or not the assumed authority is in fact real. We must have some relief."[39]

In the end, under dubious legal authority, the OSM did acquire the three properties. Nevertheless, this internal OSM conflict illustrates how questionable information was often passed on to Centralia residents as fact, only to be questioned, modified, or retracted down the road. The decentralized nature of decision-making on such issues, and the lack of clear legislation and precedent, was largely to blame. Understandably, Centralians were frustrated by and suspicious of the working of government. On the other hand, the government was so removed from the residents' perceptions that, while recognizing that Centralians were unhappy about the course of events, officials did not see themselves as a major source of the dissatisfaction.

This point is made forcefully by two documents. The first is an OSM position paper written as preparation for the September 29-30 public meeting. It reads in part: "After 18 years the residents of Centralia are disgusted, frustrated, confused, angry, and exceedingly emotional. Recognizing the volatile nature of this situation, OSM has sought at all times to be totally candid with the community. We have made no commitments we couldn't keep and we have met all the commitments we have made; thus our credibility has been established with the people and the elected officials."[40] Evidence to the contrary exists in a letter to the OSM's director from a state Department of Environmental Resources official: "Dozens of letters and phone calls to this office

seeking technical data and interpretation of the monitoring programs have evidenced both a lack of communication between
the Office of Surface Mine, U.S. Bureau of Mines and the residents, and questionable credibility of the data that is published. Consequently, OSM's credibility is rapidly declining in
the area."[41]

Or, in the words of one Centralian: "You have experts—and
you put in quotes when I say 'experts'—that work for the government . . . they won't tell you what the truth is." His wife
added, "This is why people become disinterested. Why should
we go listen to this story? We heard three others and they were
all different. What's going to make the fourth one any better or
any truer?"

Indeed, over time, some Centralians came to view themselves
as being exploited by, rather than helped by, government; they
felt caught in the middle of a power struggle between the OSM
and the Bureau of Mines.[42] The father whose hospitalized daughter was advised not to return home because of low oxygen levels
suspected that political considerations were responsible for the
delay in solving the CO_2 problems.[43] In our August 1982 survey
of adult Centralians, the vast majority indicated that government
at all levels had not done a good job of handling the problem,
and one-third of the residents in fact believed that a conspiracy
was afoot to keep the fire burning.

Although much of the negative view of government can be
attributed to problems of communication and to characteristic
bureaucratic delays, blatantly political considerations were sometimes to blame. Some government agencies and elected officials
viewed Centralia in light of their own interests and agendas.
Elected officials who represented Centralia were more likely to
attempt to push for the politically popular solution, since their
jobs depended on their perceived response. Appointed rather
than elected, agency officials generally were not concerned with
political popularity. Whatever an agency's interests were perceived to be shaped the agency's response to a given situation;

therefore, technical agencies were more likely to seek a minimal solution and to fight with the others over responsibility and turf.

Beyond the politics of the fire itself, Centralia had become involved in a controversy over "who is running Columbia County,"[44] in the words of one county commissioner. The Columbia County Redevelopment Authority (CCRA) had been assigned administrative responsibility for a Department of Housing and Urban Development grant intended for physical improvements in Centralia. The Columbia County commissioners protested that funds slated to go to the CCRA would be wasted. In June 1980, an OSM official was surprisingly candid in an internal memo that explained what had taken place during a telephone conversation with a county official: "Mr. McCracken and I further discussed the real reason, i.e. political, for the County Commissioners' actions." The memo put the conversation into this context: "The Commissioners do not want HUD Monies to be spent in Centralia which they are convinced will be razed eventually. They have asked the authority to divert these funds to other parts of the county. For its part, the authority asked HUD Philadelphia for guidance and was instructed to use funds allotted to Centralia in Centralia. This aroused the ire of the County Commissioners who were clearly of the opinion that the authority should be responsive to the Commissioners' requests rather than going to HUD."

As it turned out, the Columbia County commissioners were correct in their assessment of Centralia's fate, but such an outcome was far from most people's minds in 1980. Attention was focused once more on finding a final solution when the Bureau of Mines in September issued its long-awaited report on the status of the fire and on eleven possible solutions.[45] It was discussed at a public meeting of over 300 people on September 29-30. The option that the bureau seemed to favor called for excavating part of the burning ground and constructing two isolation trenches, at a proposed cost of $32.4 million. The September meeting was told that the OSM was evaluating the data, and that the Secretary of the Interior would make a decision on a final mine fire abatement plan by January 1, 1981.[46]

By early December, however, the OSM was backing away from its commitment to come up with a plan by January 1. One OSM official stated, "I've got no idea when a decision on an option will be made. It depends. I can't speculate."[47]

Centralians saw themselves as pawns, "shuffled through the bureaucracy" with "nobody to make a decision or take the responsibility." One resident accused the state and federal governments of "playing a form of Russian roulette. . . . Somebody's taking a gamble with our lives."

On the one hand, residents accepted the government's technical definition of the problem, which meant that the extremely elusive controllability of the fire became the central issue. On the other hand, technical knowhow failed them, and the competing interests of the various sectors of government aggravated Centralia's social problems. For eighteen years, the crisis had only worsened. After almost two decades, the fire seemed to be out of control, and government, whether by design or ineptitude, had proved incapable of dealing with it. The dilemma in Centralia parallels that of other cases where, as Gephart points out, managerial activity itself caused an environmental disaster or aggravated an existing one.[48]

As in most cases of prolonged threat, tension and stress ate away at the ability to cope.[49] How dangerous was the fire? What might it destroy? Nobody seemed to know. Diffused feelings of anxiety and demoralization were pervasive as Centralians faced the kind of threat with which it is most difficult to cope, "the generalized dread of the unknown."[50]

3. Ambiguous Evidence and Contradictory Signals

Most people who are caught in a hurricane or a tornado describe the experience as something recognized, as foreknown, even though it may in fact have been their first encounter with such a disaster. Beyond the immediate community, even those who do not experience the disaster themselves share with the survivors a common definition of the calamity. The consensus of the community and outside agencies in defining the event as a disaster encourages a coordinated response within the town. Neighbor works with neighbor to rebuild, and resources outside the town are mobilized according to established disaster policies of government and other organizations, providing relief to the survivors and help in rebuilding.[1]

Reactions to the Centralia mine fire were at wide variance from the typical communal response to an immediate-impact disaster. Contradictory differences, selectively perceived, in the sensory, emotional, and cultural evidence of the underground fire justified Centralians' use of their own varying experiences to discredit the claims of others. The rhetoric of everyday life alone ("They're seeking personal gain or power" or "They're hysterical or stupid") armed disputants with the means to explain how others could hold their convictions in the face of convincing evidence that the world is otherwise.[2] The shifting, elusive nature of the fire as a physical phenomenon bred misunderstanding among the village residents.[3]

As a matter of fact, only a handful of people have ever seen the Centralia mine fire, which is burning two to three hundred feet beneath the earth's surface. In the spring of 1981 and again in the spring of 1983, the fire did reveal itself on the surface. The 1981 "breakout," which occurred just outside the borough, in Conyngham Township, was quickly backfilled with fly ash by Pennsylvania's Department of Environmental Resources. In 1983, the fire surfaced at the bottom of a ravine about one mile from the borough. Since the path to the edge of the ravine is almost vertical, only those in good physical condition could have hiked to see the emergent fire, but even those who can lay claim to have seen the Centralia mine fire cannot say they saw it in Centralia. The 1983 breakout, like the earlier one, occurred outside the borough. That a mine fire exists, very few will argue. That there is a mine fire under Centralia remained a point of contentious debate.

"Some people refuse to believe that a fire exists in town even though it broke to the surface at one point and spews carbon monoxide everywhere," said a fifty-year-old man whose home is in the officially designated impact zone. "They refuse to even acknowledge that objectionable odor." On the other hand, in the words of a thirty-six-year-old woman living on the north end, or "cold side," of town (in reality only a little more than a half mile from her neighbor in the impact zone): "I don't believe the mine fire is in Centralia itself. I think the people just want to move. Maybe the fumes are in the houses, I don't know; that's what they're yelling about, but the fire is going the other way."

While no one has seen the mine fire in the Borough of Centralia, there is sensory evidence that its existence has affected some residents in the community. On days when the wind was blowing from the south, a mixture of carbon dioxide and sulphur dioxide—emitted from "conditioned" coal, or anthracite burning at temperatures above 200°F—rolled off the hill at St. Ignatius Church and traveled three to four blocks into the community before dissipating. For residents living in the path of the gases, there was clearly something "in the air." A mother of two small children describes her experiences of the gases: "I get very upset when I look out our front window and see the smoke coming up about three blocks from us."

Burning eyes, the taste of sulfur, and an acrid odor accompanied by headaches, lassitude, and respiratory troubles were unequivocal evidence for residents on the "hot side," or south end of town, that the gases caused by the fire were circulating in the borough. For residents on the north side of town, however, gas was not "in the air." Unless they traveled through the hot side on a day when CO_2 and SO_2 were detectable by the senses, they had to depend upon their neighbors' accounts for evidence. It was possible, of course, for residents on the cold side of town, having no personal experience of the fumes, to discredit or diminish the claims of their neighbors that hazardous gases were present.

Or, with the help of official intelligence, they might claim that the gases were not related to the mine fire, as happened in the spring of 1980, after an eight-year-old girl was hospitalized with pneumonia. Her attending physician cautioned against returning the child to her home on the south side of Centralia until the high concentration of CO_2 was reduced and the quality of ambient air was restored.[4] The OSM responded by declaring a site "emergency" and permanently relocating three families whose south-side homes were labeled health hazards. Here, surely, was indisputable evidence that the mine fire was a readily identifiable crisis demanding concerted community action. A child had been seriously ill, an "emergency" was declared, and families were forced to relocate, all because of the gas.

But, although the OSM acted quickly in declaring the houses unsafe and relocating residents, the agency was also quick to take the official position that the CO_2 was not connected with the Centralia mine fire. Carbon dioxide, the OSM stated, was a byproduct of past mining practices still present in the abandoned mines and passageways crisscrossing the underside of Centralia. The location of the three evacuated homes, on top of the highest underground temperatures in the borough, was not considered in the agency's official statement. Three years later, the Pennsylvania Department of Health was to list carbon dioxide, along with carbon monoxide and methane, as a hazardous gas that "must be addressed in relationship to the Centralia mine fire."[5]

Nevertheless, when the OSM officially separated the CO_2 from the mine fire, it denied credibility to those residents whose synchronous experience of the gas and the underground fire was to them sufficient evidence that the two were closely linked, while supporting those residents who preferred to deny the threat of the mine fire. Adopting the official position, the nay-sayers could express sympathy for families affected by the gas, but deny any relationship to the underground fire, a more catastrophic possibility. Those residents who experienced the fire mainly in terms of the official government interpretation drew one set of conclusions, whereas the Centralians whose senses experienced the gas in living on top of the hot area came to very different conclusions. Divided between two groups who experienced the world in very different ways, the community was unlikely to arrive at a definitive version of "what really was happening."

A more insidious gaseous product of the mine fire was virtually undetectable by the Centralians themselves. Unlike CO_2 and SO_2, which can be registered by sight, taste, smell, and physical reactions, the deadly carbon monoxide is detectable only by gas monitors. Colorless, odorless, tasteless, and non-irritating, CO is formed whenever a carbon-based fuel is incompletely burned. Considered by the Pennsylvania Department of Health to be the most dangerous side effect of the underground mine fire, CO combines with the hemoglobin in the blood, interfering with the blood's capacity to carry oxygen to the cells of the body. Acute CO poisoning ends in death by respiratory failure.

In a 1967 accident in the town of Shamokin, a fifteen-mile drive from Centralia, five people had died in their sleep of CO poisoning caused by an underground mine fire. That accident was on the minds of many Centralians whose homes fell within the area that the U.S. Bureau of Mines in 1982 called the impact zone.[6] The hazards of CO from mine fires were familiar to most Centralians.

In the early 1980s, the Bureau of Mines funded a project to monitor air quality in homes to assure that the safety of residents was not jeopardized by the seepage of dangerous gases. This project, typical of the imperfections in the government's hazard management policies, ended up as little more than a source of community discord. The Pennsylvania Department of Environmental Resources (DER), appointed to monitor homes, surveyed the entire community in the winter of 1981. DER representatives knocked on doors and asked residents if they wanted gas monitors placed in their homes, an inspector to check their homes regularly for gases, or both. Only nine families outside the impact zone requested a routine check of their homes for gases. Not one family outside the impact zone requested a monitor.

Within the impact zone, sixteen households and St. Ignatius School were the first to sign up for the gas detectors. In the course of the next several weeks, more hot-side families accepted the government's offer. In all, 72 of the 106 families living in the impact zone, or 69 percent, requested the devices.

The DER recommended that the monitors be placed in the basement, since the mine gases were most likely to enter a house through the basement floor. The black monitors, each with a large red bell on one side, were designed for industrial use in deep mines, not for residences. Each device, measuring 22 by 10 by 9 inches, emitted a clucking sound, at roughly 70 clucks per minute. Despite the ominous sight and sound of the large black boxes, and contrary to the government's advice, most Centralians wanted the monitors placed in the living areas of their homes, saying that it made them feel safer. The family room, dining room, and hallways were the most frequent spots for the clucking black box. One or two DER inspectors would enter most homes daily, to take carbon monoxide readings from the monitors and to spot-check drains and faucets for traces of carbon dioxide and methane.

The obtrusive presence of the monitors in the living areas of their homes and the daily appearance of the DER inspectors made most families on the hill feel haunted by the persistent threat of gas poisoning. Comparatively few residences were found to have gas levels that exceeded the standards for ambient air used by the DER, but many families complained of the symptoms that accompany chronic exposure to higher than normal levels of CO and CO_2. Over time, many families expressed distrust of the DER monitoring program, suspicious of a cover-up. Residents wondered out loud how they could feel so poorly when they were inside their homes if the air was safe to breathe, as the DER claimed it was. For many residents, the gases were experienced in ways inconsistent with the official interpretation that the gas problem was a potential, not an actual, threat.

Centralians who believed the gases posed an immediate and real threat to their health could find support for their fears when they picked up the local daily newspaper. In March of 1981, the paper reported the views of a "distinguished" medical researcher on the adverse health effects of chronic exposure to low levels of CO.[7] Citing danger at threshold figures well below those set by the DER, the scientist confirmed the sensory experiences of many residents, who complained of chronic colds, fatigue, headaches, and various other ailments. Another official voice was thus added to the growing babel of scientists, legislators, attorneys, and social service personnel seeking to make themselves heard as Centralians sought to make sense of the mine fire and organize their reactions to it.

In contrast to residents of the impact zone, most residents who lived as far away as the fringes of the hot-side area or at the north end of town were not confronted by an immediate threat of poisonous gases and the daily presence of environmental inspectors. Without sensory affirmation in the form of physical symptoms, a gas monitor, or visits from the DER inspectors, residents could simply ignore the gas problem, which many did; or they could see the claims of their neighbors on the hill as the product of unrealistic fear or as a conspiracy to get rich quick by selling their homes to the government at inflated prices. Consider the reasoning of a middle-aged man who lived at the far north end of town: "Some people are using the problems [associated with the fire] to achieve personal gains. And the news media are always highlighting whatever those people have to say to make them look like no one else cares and they are representing the town. Well, they're not representing me or the town as far as I'm concerned. They're looking out for themselves."

For the Centralians who lived on the hill, the suspicions that their experiences of fear and dread were manipulative displays or an inaccurate perception of reality were cruel character judgments that denied their fundamental right to a safe, healthy environment. Disputes over underlying motives, typical of the community's response to its crisis, could not be reconciled simply by determining whether or not gases were in fact seeping into homes.

Beyond the disjuncture over mine gases, the community also split over the threat of subsidence, as miners call cave-ins. Subsidence occurs when heat from a mine fire burns rock substrata, so weakening the support for the ground's surface that it literally caves in, leaving a hole anywhere from a foot to several yards in diameter. Subsidence may also be the result of mining more than twice. During a third mining, the underground pillars supporting the mine shaft are "robbed," leaving only a few feet of topsoil as a ceiling over a sizable cavern. The thin layer of soil is likely to give way under the weight of vehicular traffic, heavy rainfall, or even pedestrians. Most of the pillars under Centralia have been robbed.

Twelve cave-ins have been reported in Centralia since 1980. Though most of Centralia was susceptible to subsidence, all twelve occurred on the hot side of town. In specific areas understood to be at high risk, red signs warned, "Posted—Keep Out— Danger." An area about a half block square was thought to be so hazardous that it was enclosed with an 8-foot-high chain link fence.

Were the twelve subsidences on the hot side of town related to the fire? Centralians could not agree. Some reasoned that the disproportionate number of cave-ins on the hill was simply the result of having robbed a greater number of pillars from that area. If more third mining had occurred in that area, they reasoned, then subsidences were more likely. Other Centralians,

however, particularly those living on the hill, were convinced
that the twelve cave-ins were tied directly to the mine fire, and
that anyone who thought otherwise couldn't see what was really
going on.

Even if Centralians had not been polarized by the mine gases
and the cave-ins, they might have split into factions when the
social action groups came to town. Such groups focus on a set of
specific concerns such as the environment, the plight of women,
the poor, or the victims of inept or unlawful treatment by big
government or large corporations. The heavier a social action
group's caseload, and the more problems it is working on at any
given time, the easier it is to justify further funding, thereby
ensuring its continuance. Moreover, to become involved with a
case that has captured national attention adds to the credibility
of the organization, further certifying its reason for being.[8]

It is thus not surprising that several social action groups con-
tacted organizations within Centralia to offer their services. Such
Washington, D.C.—based organizations as Rural American
Women, Ralph Nader's Public Interest Coalition, the Sierra
Club, the National Clean Air Coalition, and the Campaign for
Human Development were complemented by various Pennsyl-
vania-based groups, including the Harrisburg office of Catholic
Social Services and the Delaware Valley Citizens' Council for
Clean Air. Some of these organizations limited their contact with
the community to an exchange of letters; others became closely
associated with the town's predicament, unwittingly adding to
the conflict that divided the community. Surely the motivations
of these groups had strong elements of altruism. Centralia was
part of a "cause" in which they believed. At the same time, each
group also had its own organizational interests to further.

To justify their presence in Centralia, these organizations defined the mine fire in terms consistent with the interpretations
of residents who saw the fire as an immediate threat to their
health and safety and who blamed government for failing to act
in their best interests. Thus, in the curious logic of mutual affirmation, Centralians who defined the mine fire as a menace

justified the involvement of special-interest groups which, by
their involvement, affirmed the worst fears for life and property.
And, to the extent that the special interest groups affirmed these
fears, they challenged the beliefs of other residents who held
that the fire was a mere annoyance or at most a remote risk.

Another element in the complexity that confronted Centralia
was the number of law firms and individual attorneys who sought
by various means to represent individuals and groups in lawsuits
against the government. One attorney, for example, advised a
grassroots group at a public meeting to sue the Centralia Borough
Council. When attorneys offered to represent in a court of law
those residents who interpreted the fire as a threat, they served
to corroborate the legitimacy of feeling threatened.

In all the complex and contradictory encounters Centralians
had with the mine fire, one thing is clear: no single observation
or experience of the crisis could stand as definitive; every position
had at least some discreditors. Centralians thus found themselves
in the unusually difficult position of having to piece together
their own individual accounts of what the mine fire meant and
what, if anything, should be done to help their community.

The many individual interpretations of the underground mine
fire fractured the established social alignments in Centralia and
aroused anger and resentment among neighbors and friends. The
different meanings that people assigned to the fire, and the emotive freight those differences carried, depended on the residents'
perceptions of the risks posed by the subsurface conflagration.
Many families in Centralia perceived the poisonous gases and
the threat of subsidence as hazardous agents with a high degree
of physical risk. One woman claimed to have kept an "emergency
suitcase containing valuables and necessities under the bed and
a pet carrier nearby in the event of a disaster." Other families
saw the risks posed by the fire as having a low probability of
endangering their health or well-being. In the words of a young
man living next to the impact zone: "The fire and gases may
reach this far. I don't know. Right now I'm in the clear." Still
other families conducted their lives as if the fire was at most an

annoyance, hardly a risk. Unlike the therapeutic community that
emerges in the wake of immediate-impact disasters, the product
of chronic technological disasters such as the Centralia mine fire
is likely to be multiple groups, who experience and interpret the
ecological threat as a concern to "us" and not to "them," or to
"them" and not "us."

Many Centralians who felt themselves to be at high risk responded to the threat of the gases and subsidence through informal gatherings around kitchen tables or, more formally, by
joining an organized group. On such collective occasions, their
fears were reinforced and intensified; the perception of imminent
danger and the need to respond became more important than
the preservation of the community. Under the conditions of collective stress, individuals detached themselves from any commitment to the town. In fact, many of these residents perceived
the community as an obstacle in their efforts to find some relief
from the dangers posed by the fire.

Understandably, those Centralians who perceived the risks
posed by the fire to be low also began to perceive neighbors who
feared imminent danger as a threat to the preservation of the
community. In a community where 47 percent of the residents
have lived in their homes twenty-five years or longer, the threat
to community existence was met with dread and anger toward
neighbors who had, from the long-timers' perspective, clearly
misjudged the seriousness of the problem. Many Centralians who
saw the high-risk believers as themselves a peril to the community began to organize to "save their town."

Thus emerged what many perceived as two irreconcilable
goals: the preservation of health and safety, and the preservation
of Centralia. For most residents who would become involved in
the conflict, achievement of one goal meant sacrificing the other.
Since the stakes were high, the dissension left little room for
compromise, and since the evidence was equivocal, contradictory, and vague, even contradictory interpretations were officially and experientially confirmed.

Under some circumstances, conflict can serve to solidify a

group.[9] The conflict that emerged in Centralia, however, did not strengthen the consensual bases of the community; it put the assumption of basic consensus in question. Centralians did not resolve their differences on the basis of an underlying unity; quite the contrary, they splintered on the basis of their differences. Fragmented at its core, the community could not generate collective pressure on the state and federal agencies to respond promptly and competently to the crisis. What social energy there was expressed itself in the form of mutual opposition, or "tension without action—a form of social paralysis."[10]

4. A Group Emerges and the Town Divides

Taking their cue from the hostage crisis in Iran, several residents on the south end of Centralia began to think of their predicament as being parallel to the forceful, illegal detaining of Americans in a hostile environment. One family painted a sign, roughly 3 feet by 3 feet, worded "Mine Fire Holds Families Hostage!!!" and secured it to a fence next to the street for all to see.

In January 1981, the warning device on the carbon monoxide monitor in one Centralia home started sounding almost every other day, alerting the family by a loud, persistent ring that the air in their home was hazardous to their health. But not until three weeks later, on February 9, did the Pennsylvania Department of Health list the home as unsafe because of higher than acceptable levels of carbon monoxide.

Although that home was the third in Centralia where high CO levels warranted an official declaration of the hazard, no state or federal funds were made available to help families in relocating. At the time, the only assistance forthcoming from government agencies was advice to "ventilate" their "unsafe" homes by opening the windows. This advice was the first hard evidence for many families living on the hill that official declarations were not necessarily followed by official actions. They shared their feelings of vulnerability and entrapment around kitchen tables and over the phone.

On February 14, 1981, a twelve-year-old boy narrowly escaped death in Centralia when the ground he was walking on collapsed under him. In his words, "I just sort of started sinking down, down to my knees, then down to my waist, then I went all the way down."[1] Grabbing desperately for anything to break his fall, his fingers found the root of a tree protruding from the side of the mine cave-in. He clung to it, literally for life. His screams for help alerted his nearby cousin, who managed to pull him to safety. Later in the day a DER inspector recorded a temperature of 350°F in the pit, and the CO level exceeded the scale on the inspector's gas detector. Borough of Centralia officials reported that had the boy remained in the hole for longer than three minutes, he would have died.[2]

This near-fatality occurred within a hundred yards of the three homes declared unsafe by the Department of Health. Ironically, as the earth was collapsing under the boy, state and federal legislators and several government scientists were across the street inspecting one of the homes plagued by toxic gases. On learning of the incident, one of the state legislators appealed to the governor of Pennsylvania to declare a state of emergency in Centralia. The governor decided against this course of action but appointed a task force to review the community's predicament.

Less than four weeks after the near-fatality, a sixty-three-year-old man was overcome by carbon monoxide in one of the three homes across the street that were listed as unsafe. Unconscious, he was rushed to a hospital where emergency staff revived him with oxygen. When DER inspectors measured the oxygen level in the man's home, they found it to be dangerously low. Within a week of the incident, the man's family was moved from its home of twenty-eight years to a trailer several blocks away, provided by the Pennsylvania Emergency Management Agency.

A child's narrow escape from a searing gaseous pit, an elderly man's near-asphyxiation, the health department's advice that the windows of unsafe houses be kept open rather than relocating families, for which no money was available—these events pushed angry, frightened residents toward one another. Some citizens felt that the costs of the Centralia mine fire were being meted out in a high degree of personal risk and the progressive deterioration of both the environment and the community. Such a toll, they assumed, would be reason enough for residents of a small town to forget their differences and unite to protect one another and their way of life.

Such was the perception of the first citizens' group to organize in response to the mine fire. On April 9, 1981, articles of incorporation were filed in the Columbia County Courthouse for the Concerned Citizens Action Group Against the Centralia Mine Fire, called CC for short.

The CC initially understood the hazardous conditions wrought by the fire as a common problem perceived by everyone in town. Though the group was originated by Centralians who saw their health and safety as being in immediate danger, the founding members believed they would receive the support of the wider community. Surely, they reasoned, any competent witness to reality would arrive at the same conclusion they had reached: the threats posed by the fire were unacceptable. Presuming a community of others concerned about the dangers they were experiencing, the CC assumed that no one in town could define the crisis in terms other than those used by the group. "We just thought everybody would join up, or most people anyways," mused one of the founding members of the organization.

Nothing could have been further from the truth. The CC was quickly identified by other Centralians as a renegade band bent on destroying the placid, tranquil life of their community. "Get rid of Concerned Citizens," railed one man. "They're making our town look like a three-ring circus." "Nobody can agree on nothing in this town," said an elderly woman, "because the Concerned Citizens open their big mouths all the time and never know what they're talking about."

At the heart of the discord between the two sides lay different perceptions of the immediacy of the risk. Although our 1982 community survey revealed that 67 percent of adult Centralians felt that their health or safety was at some degree of risk because of the mine fire, proximity to the fire influenced the perception of how immediate the risks were. For example, 23 percent of those living outside the impact zone agreed that "the mine fire is just not as dangerous as most people think," while only 14 percent of impact zone residents were in agreement. Concerning their own safety, 49 percent of cold-side adults felt no threat from the fire, while only 22 percent of hot-side residents felt safe. At the opposite extreme, a sense of being "very threatened" was expressed by only 17 percent of those living on the cold side, but by 36 percent of impact zone residents.

In other words, Centralians tended to evaluate the chance of being harmed by the fire according to where they lived in the borough. Those living outside the impact zone perceived a potential danger to themselves and the community from the mine fire, but the risk was seen as a remote problem, to be tolerated while government engineers worked out a plan for relieving the dangers. Risk remained an individual issue, a relatively infrequent topic of conversation. On the other hand, many of the impact zone inhabitants perceived danger to be a fact and risk an urgent problem requiring an immediate solution. The immediacy of their experiences of the fire pushed the hot-siders toward one another, setting the stage for the founding of the CC.

The contrasting risk assessments of cold-side and hot-side residents were expressed in the thirty-eight conversational interviews conducted during this study. In twenty of these interviews, Centralians who lived outside the area of town designated dangerous all recognized the threat posed by the mine fire, acknowledging with varying degrees of certainty their personal concern about its catastrophic potential. But not one of these cold-siders identified the risks as immediate. In the words of a woman living at the far north end of the borough: "That fire has a mind of its own. You know, it's outsmarted the government for years. What's stopping it from burning right under our home? . . . I don't have the problems some of those families have up on Park and Locust Streets. And I don't want them."

An elderly man living on the west end of town, who had pneumoconiosis, or "black lung disease," brought on by work in the mines, feared that gases from the fire might seep into his home and aggravate his breathing problems. To assuage his fear that the gases might be threatening his health, he periodically called the local DER office to hear in the reassuring words of the inspector that the gases were potentially hazardous only for residents living "on the hill." "As long as they tell me it's 'on the hill,' " the elderly man reasoned, "I can live with it."

A forty-two-year-old man living on the west side was personally concerned about the fire "only to the extent that I have vague suspicions that it's detrimental to my health sometimes when I walk around the place, because of a cardiac condition." The same man "put severe restrictions" on his eight-year-old son, denying him permission to ride his bicycle on the hot side of town: "Oh yes, I will not allow him to Park Street and beyond. He knows this, he respects it. For what it's worth, I've threatened him literally with a licking if he goes up there . . . I don't want him anywhere near there."

In these and other ways, Centralians living outside the impact zone made minor adjustments in routine to manage whatever potential risks they saw in the fire. Their individual perceptions of any threat as being relatively remote precluded collective action.

For many hot-side inhabitants, however, the fire represented an immediate threat to their health and well-being that pushed them toward a collective response. The hot-siders felt powerless to reduce the threat to manageable proportions and doubted the government's ability to help them avoid the fire's consequences. They interpreted the mine fire in terms quite different from those of their neighbors across town.[3] An eighty-two-year-old woman admitted to being "afraid of the gases and afraid of subsidences." By that point, she was also "tired of being afraid . . . and the government's no help either. They don't seem to care, and when they do do something, it doesn't seem to help."

"My home is not safe, my yard is not safe, my town is not safe, and no one does anything about it," declared a thirty-two-year-old mother of two. "My children have great cases of respiratory infections. We have emotional problems in our family. . . . It [the mine fire] has affected us greatly."

A middle-aged man described his personal responses to living in the impact zone in this way: "I don't lay awake at night worrying about it, but I do worry about it quite a bit. I do have gases in my home, and I keep thinking, Oh my God, my brain cells. I forgot something. Is it because of the gases? I go to bed and I think, Oh, I wonder if I'll wake up tomorrow morning."

"Scared, that's what I am," explained a fifty-eight-year-old woman. "My brother had to move out of town because his home was full of gas. When I went down and seen them moving, I cried my heart out, because they were very close to me. I felt bad, but I never dreamt that the government wasn't going to do something to stop it [the fire] before it came to us. Now here it is in my backyard. You know, my mother and father died of cancer, and I think the gases are going to give me a cancer."

An immediate risk demands more than minor, individual adjustments in routine. Frightened and unsure of how to cope on a day-to-day basis with the threat of the fire, many of the hotside inhabitants began to seek out others who felt the same, taking comfort in the knowledge that they were not alone. Gradually, over the course of several informal meetings, the idea of an organized response to the crisis emerged. Simply in the act of creating the organization, the founding members of the CC reduced uncertainty and took the opportunity to help one another manage the tensions associated with life in the impact zone.

But of deeper significance was the emergence of a shared set of assumptions concerning the extent and kinds of danger CC members and their families were facing. Over time, these assumptions acquired permanence supported by personal commitment, becoming a belief system that would serve CC members both in appraising threatening circumstances and in acting as a group. Because the beliefs focused on danger and the threat of loss, we refer to these linked assumptions as a threat belief system.[4]

Whereas risk perception can be understood as part of an individual's personal reality, a threat belief system is a supraindividual, or cultural, phenomenon. Quite unlike an individual's risk perception, threat belief systems constitute paradigms for *collective* action.[5] Organizational life takes place in the name of these belief systems. Members of the new group that emerged in Centralia regulated their conduct and explained their behavior on the basis of a set of beliefs about the extent and nature of the danger that a disaster agent posed for them, their families, and their community. The emergence of this new group, with ideas about the quality of community life and the safety of the local environment that differed radically from those of their neighbors, polarized social relations in the town.

The failure of the CC to appeal to a representative portion of the town was also related to the generational differences between the group's members and other residents. CC members were primarily young or middle-aged adults with children. In a town where close to 60 percent of the adults were more than fifty years old and 40 percent were more than sixty-two years old, the typical CC member was considered young. The designation "young" often carried, in Centralia, the added meanings of impulsive, heedless, and brash. It was not infrequent to hear others in town refer to the CC as a "young bunch of hotheads" who lacked a sense of responsibility or proper regard for the consequences of their actions.

A seventy-six-year-old man attributed divisiveness in the town to "a certain element who wants to get a lot of money and move. They are the young Concerned Citizens, who never saw a mine." A sixty-one-year-old retired miner rejected the CC as being "mostly too young to know much about mining and mine fires." In the words of a seventy-one-year-old woman: "The Concerned Citizens are acting like greedy children. Give them some money to get out of town. That's all they want." Dismissing the CC in this fashion precluded a thoughtful consideration of their predicament and made it impossible to consider seriously the claims of the organization.

Several members of the CC responded in kind to the remarks of their senior neighbors, emphasizing the generational differences. From a twenty-three-year-old CC member: "Our biggest problem are the older people in town who are ignorant of the dangers of the fire and are too stubborn to leave their homes."

A young father of two found the older people "too comfortable in their homes and too old to give a damn [about us]."

The demographic differences between the CC and a majority of the town's residents led not only to name-calling, but also to significant differences in attitude toward the fire. With their children raised and gone, with an emotional commitment to their homes and neighborhood as a good place to live out their remaining years, Centralia's elderly were less inclined to interpret the fire as a life-threatening crisis demanding a quick solution—particularly if that solution would unsettle their way of life. In interviews and on public occasions, several of Centralia's elderly expressed the desire to be left alone to live, as one man phrased it, "those years God has left for me in peace."

For the members of the CC, however, there was plenty of life yet to be lived. There were children to raise and careers to pursue. As they interpreted it, the fire had already unsettled their way of living, had indeed endangered their very lives. For them the situation was intolerable.

Clearly, geographic proximity to the fire was a major variable in distinguishing those prepared to believe the worst from those who interpreted the fire as a minor annoyance. But even within the impact zone, generational factors differentially encouraged the quest for information about the fire and predisposed some residents to fashion these data into a coherent interpretation of what was happening.

The threat belief system of the CC did not develop slowly, over the several months of the group's existence. Even by the time of the organization's first formal meeting, the outlines of the belief system were common knowledge to most of the original membership. In fact, it could be argued that the basis of the founding members' original attraction to one another was their common set of threat beliefs regarding the scope and seriousness of the fire. As an organization, the CC served to intensify those beliefs and to disseminate them within and outside the borough.

Because the founding members of the CC had constructed a

meaningful interpretation of their predicament before the group even existed, the CC did not encourage alternative interpretations of the dangers posed by the fire. Indeed, alternative interpretations were considered heresy by the core members, who were passionately concerned with convincing others that their beliefs were the only logical and morally correct positions. In the minds of CC members, people who disagreed with them were either ill-informed (they didn't live close enough to the fire to see its effects) or lying (they had some ulterior motive for making false claims). This intolerance of alternative interpretations was at the root of some of the problems the CC was to face.

The fervor with which CC members expressed their beliefs arose in part from their identification with the most severely affected families. It is true that personal experience of toxic gases or the subsidence above mine workings helped to shape the threat beliefs, but the fire did not create hazardous conditions for every resident of Centralia, and the hazardous conditions that existed varied in the degree of danger, with some families experiencing a single incident of elevated gas readings and others subject to repeated or continuous incidents. Not everyone who held the threat beliefs could recount personal experiences to confirm the legitimacy and intensity of the danger, and even personal encounters with the fire varied in number and intensity. But their shared assumptions about the danger of the fire had their sources in accredited public information: the worst-case experiences of several families who lived in homes with persistently high gas readings and the crisis events that occurred on the hill.[6]

Interviews and discussions with the founding members of the CC suggest that those families most jeopardized by the mine gases and the subsidences became reference points when others on the hill wanted to make some sense out of the type and degree of risk to which they and their families might be exposed. The severe, atypical cases were frequently talked about as if they were the common experience—as if the most extreme were also the most representative.[7] For example, when dangers associated with the fire were the topic of conversation, it was the testimony of those whose homes had been declared unsafe by the state Department of Health, and the experiences of others who would be offered relocation money in 1981, that served as points of reference. In formal testimony during a hearing in Centralia of the Mines and Energy Committee of the state House of Representatives, the most severely affected residents reported on their experiences of the fire and the gases. The worst-case experiences of the fire were used as evidence by others on the hill to affirm their interpretation of the problem:

When you look at TV, next thing you know [you wake up and] an hour and a half has gone by and the program is over. If any one of you have any trouble sleeping at night . . . all you have to do is come to my apartment and sit there and I guarantee you you'll fall asleep.

A Bureau of Mines representative told us a home could be checked out ok when the inspector comes in the morning, but that afternoon a strong surge of gas could come and kill every living thing in the house. Nobody knows when that surge is going to come. . . . It's really scary.

Today, my [carbon monoxide] monitor alarm sounded three times, and now carbon monoxide is in my home. The time for being complacent and hoping for a miracle is over.[8]

The worst-case families served as reference groups even after they had been relocated, and even though no gas levels of comparable magnitude were recorded in any of the other homes in Centralia.[9]

Moreover, the two most dramatic effects of the fire, the subsidence that the twelve-year-old boy fell into and the carbon monoxide gas that overcame an elderly man, were evoked by the original CC members most frequently when the subject turned to how dangerous it was to live on the hill: "What happened to [the man overcome by gas]—and we can only thank God, and the rescue boys, that he is not dead—could happen to anybody living on top of this fire." "A young lad almost lost his life and the kids are getting sick because of these mine gases. . . . It's like the government is waiting for someone to die before they say, 'Hey, this mine fire is serious.' "

Only the most extreme and statistically unrepresentative cases served as the standards by which other, perhaps less severely affected, families were to evaluate their own living conditions. Presentiments of loss or harm from the fire were founded on the relatively few catastrophic events and obvious threats in the history of the blaze, not on the long and tedious chronology of events that might have encouraged a less dreadful apprehension of the crisis. It is not hard to account for the significance that some residents attributed to the dramatic events in town. A mine fire generates as much uncertainty as it does gases—prolonged uncertainty about the high-stakes issues of health and safety and economic well-being. Even though extreme cases may be statistically unrepresentative of residents' experiences to date, there is no way of calculating the statistical probability of harm in the future. Hot-side residents, uncertain as to what dangers might befall them, naturally feared the worst, and they reinforced each other's threat beliefs through CC activities and informal gatherings. Ironically, the construction and dissemination of this threat belief system only heightened the fear and hostility. On the one hand, CC members became ever more convinced that their worst fears would inevitably come to pass; on the other, cold-side residents viewed the CC as responding hysterically to an unfounded account of danger.

The local newspaper's coverage of the fire reinforced the threat beliefs of the CC. Our survey indicated that fully 90 percent of the people living in Centralia received information about the fire from the local newspaper.[10] In fact, the paper became part of the divisive struggle between Centralians. Opinions of the paper's trustworthiness, for example, differed dramatically, depending on attitude toward the fire. Of the 67 percent of Centralians who thought their safety was at least somewhat threatened by the fire, 62 percent believed that the information they received from the paper about the fire was accurate. Indeed, the founding members of the CC saw the paper as a credible, unbiased source of information, critical to their efforts to cope with the hazards of the fire. On the other hand, only 38 percent of the Centralians who did not feel threatened were confident of the accuracy of what the newspaper printed. Many of these residents saw the paper as exaggerating the dangers of the situation and taking sides with the CC against the rest of the community.

In the first few weeks of 1981, the editorial board of the newspaper decided to "bring the town's plight to national attention and to help the townspeople."[11] The paper's coverage before that time, however, indicates that the paper was moving toward an advocate role for residents on the hill well before the editorial board's announced decision to publicize the issue. As early as December 12, 1979, the paper printed an editorial accusing the federal Office of Surface Mining of a "do-nothing attitude" about the mine fire and a lack of concern for the health and safety of Centralians. The editorial criticized the inability of the OSM to decide what to do about the growing threat from the underground fire.

The latest development is the fire forced the closing of a gasoline service station as a safety precaution. Heat generated by the . . . fire warmed the ground beneath the station, a threat to the gasoline-filled tanks, which were emptied. . . . If gasoline-filled tanks are hazardous, the [natural gas] pipeline is even more of a threat to the safety of community and its residents. . . . To say the entire community is in jeopardy is not overstating the situation. . . . Another certainty is the fire has the potential for serious, if not tragic consequences."[12]

Two themes in this editorial would serve the paper in the coming months as the primary foci in its coverage of the fire: the failure of government agencies and legislators to find a response to the disaster, and the growing peril to health and well-being, particularly for families living on the hill. Repetition of these themes would intensify the perceptions of many Centralians on the south end that they lived from day to day with imminent disaster and could expect little help from the government, which appeared to have no control over what was happening.

The paper relied heavily on reporting worst-case situations in carrying out its stated intention of bringing the plight of Centralia to national attention. The persistent emphasis on dangerous, chaotic, irrational happenings made them appear, to Centralians predisposed to believe the worst, to be typical consequences of the fire.[13]

In its studied concern with the extreme case, the local paper made regular use of the human interest story. Within a couple of weeks of the first organized meeting of the CC, the local paper ran a four-part series on families who lived in homes with the most serious levels of toxic gases, where gas monitors were registering excessive levels of carbon monoxide almost daily. These conditions were not typical of Centralia, and in any case the families, along with more than two dozen others, were about to be relocated at the government's expense. In such articles as "Family's Nightmare Ending," however, the newspaper emphasized the dramatic. Identifying carbon monoxide as "a lethal gas in heavy concentrations and a health destroyer . . . in lesser ones," the article describes a "nerve shattering alarm" and portrays the efforts of the family to "combat the gas." It ends on an editorial note: "The federal government will demolish his home after the family leaves and the mine fire will have the last laugh." Two days later, the story "Gas Victim 'Free At Last' " depicted the plight of another family in similarly vivid language.[14]

In late March 1981, a front-page story carried the headline "Two doctors say: mine fire gases harmful for susceptible persons."[15] The article began with a reminder of just how dangerous the situation was: "To someone living in Centralia, there are few things as frightening as the possibility that dangerous gases from the mine fire beneath the borough might some day find their way into a home and sicken or kill somebody's family—possibly one's own." The stated intent of the article was "to inform the people of Centralia about the dangers they face from the mine fire gases." Note that the intent was not to inform residents about the *possible* dangers or the *likelihood* of harm from the gases. The assumption was clearly that the residents were in fact endangered, but that not all of them were aware of just how imperiled they were: "It is well known to borough residents that high levels of carbon monoxide or carbon dioxide, low levels of oxygen—all byproducts of the mine fire—can kill or cause serious illness. But they perhaps are not aware medical researchers have found that even low levels of carbon monoxide—lower than found in some Centralia homes—can cause serious health problems for certain people."

The story quotes at length a "distinguished" researcher whose studies suggest that exposure to even low levels of carbon monoxide can aggravate the condition of those predisposed to upper respiratory illnesses. According to another expert, representing the Pennsylvania Department of Health: "It is possible that a subsidence could occur in the basement of a Centralia home and allow a strong surge of carbon monoxide to enter it, possibly overcoming and killing a family before they could take notice and escape." Noting that the people of Centralia "are very, very frightened," he added, "I think I would be if I lived up there." In such stories, the "possible" was transformed to "probable." On several occasions, members of the CC referred to this article and others like it in testifying to the dangerous conditions they were forced to live with.

The media, in particular the daily that had publicly assumed an advocacy role for the most severely threatened segment of the community, were perceived as a more accurate source of information about the fire than the government experts.[16] In bringing the "plight of Centralians" to national attention, reporters were predisposed to focus on instances of government mismanagement that would confirm the belief that the experts were not in control.

The local daily also used the editorial page on a regular basis to sound the same themes. Of the twelve editorials on Centralia appearing between January 1 and April 30, 1981, nine have titles that make direct reference to danger or to government inertia and dishonesty. With few exceptions, the twelve editorials make pronouncements of imminent danger and unscrupulous government response. To cite but three examples:

Despite all their rosy promises, federal officials still show a shocking lack of sympathy for Centralians. . . . [In the meantime] the underground fire keeps burning, posing increased danger to life and property."

While the debate on the future course of the mine fire project is pursued at a snail's pace by the federal bureaucracy, people's lives remain in constant danger.

Will it take the loss of human life to persuade the federal government to step in and extinguish the fire?"[17]

In three editorials appearing February 19, March 16, and April 28, 1981, the paper pronounced the mine fire serious enough for an official declaration of disaster. Another editorial during this period warned Centralians that government delay might itself cause a disaster: "We believe that efforts to resolve the mine fire are moving too slow, and waiting . . . only courts disaster."[18] In other words, the local daily did more than just report the "facts."

Because the paper adopted a worst-case interpretation, its greatest appeal was to those residents who were also inclined to view the crisis in the most negative way—a mutually affirmative dynamic. It was the founders of the CC, a small, unrepresentative group, to whom the local reporters turned when they wanted an inside story on Centralia. It was the threat beliefs of the CC, based upon the most extreme assessment of the dangers associated with the fire, that received the most extensive coverage. Indeed, the relationship between several families on the hill and the little daily was so close that when the gas warning bells sounded, residents called the newspaper along with the DER inspector, to ensure that a reporter would be on hand to observe the inspector's visit and write it up for the next day's edition. In turn, the almost daily coverage of the hardest-hit families could only confirm the worst fears of others on the hill. Hot-siders found their extreme interpretations of the fire validated by what they understood to be a reliable, unbiased authority, an ally in their attempt to convince others of the desperate nature of their predicament.

In the view of one of the original members of the CC, the local daily "saw the problem like we saw it and told it straight." "This paper doesn't even come from our town," observed another member of the group, "but it understands what we're facing, which is more than I can say for a lot of the people that live in this town." The symbiotic relationship between the local press and the CC gained in complexity when the daily began giving information to the group several days before printing it. On more than one occasion, a reporter supplied information from sources outside the borough that served to legitimate the belief that the fire represented an imminent danger. Such information would then be used by residents to claim that, no matter what the government said, they were at risk because the official monitoring of their homes was too crude to detect the presence of low levels of poisonous gases.

To some extent, the local paper influenced regional and national coverage of the mine fire, since print or television reporters who made the trip to Centralia would seek to interview those Centralians most frequently cited in the local daily. Six men and women, four of them members of the CC, were interviewed more frequently by the extra-local media than anyone else. Such national attention added credibility to the coverage of the local press. As one man put it, "You can say the local paper plays favorites. . . . But when the same stuff is on national TV and makes the *New York Times*, you've gotta sit up straight and take notice."

Families in the impact zone, including the founders of the

CC, saw the local daily as their advocate in facing the real peril of the fire. This alliance was praised in a letter to the editor headed "A Cry For Help," signed by nine families living on the hill (five of them members of CC at some point):

What a great feeling to know our local paper is behind residents of Centralia. You showed us you care, you sympathize. The families in the impact area appreciate this.

Now if only we can get the support of our neighbors. Today I have gas [in my home], tomorrow it could be you crying out for help. . . . We need your support now.[19]

The local newspaper was not without its detractors among the many in town who did not accept the threat beliefs of the CC: "People don't know all the facts! The newspaper blows everything out of proportion to scare people." "I am fed up with the media's lies. It [the mine fire] isn't as bad as they say it is." "The real problem with this fire is the local news media reporters use this confusion to twist everything to suit themselves." Not a few of the cold-side residents explicitly linked the local paper to the CC: "The fire has bothered me and my family only due to the anxiety caused by the local newspaper and the 'Concerned Citizens.' That group should be run out of town."

In protest against the perceived bias of the paper, several Centralians at one point suggested that reporters be excluded from a proposed community meeting. The paper naturally responded by defending its coverage: "We believe that we have acted in a responsible way to call public attention to Centralia's serious problem. . . . We are sincere in our concern for the welfare and safety of Centralia residents. . . . We are not 'the enemy' or a dangerous entity that needs to be controlled."[20]

Nevertheless, on several occasions throughout the tumultuous months of 1983, the local reporter assigned to the story was barred from attending community meetings. A councilman justified the action on the grounds that "we just can't trust he'll get his facts straight." Nor was the Centralia Borough Council the only group to close some of its deliberations to the local press: of the several grassroots groups to emerge during 1983, only one permitted the press regular access to its meetings. Indeed, dissatisfaction with local coverage of the mine fire became so acute during the spring of 1983 that several Centralians, who ironically could not agree on a course of action for the town, did agree that the local paper should remove its reporter from the Centralia beat. Their appeal to the editor of the paper fell on deaf ears.[21]

The role of the local newspaper in Centralia was addressed in a feasibility study of resident relocation by the Institute on Man and Science in October 1981. The purpose of this study was to evaluate the social environment in Centralia and to determine what role the institute might play in coordinating a relocation program for the borough. Regarding the local newspaper, the institute concluded:

The fire is, of course, nationally newsworthy, so it is a big fish for a small town newspaper to have in its pages every day. The desire to make the most of such journalistic good fortune is understandable. Nevertheless, the paper has not earned a reputation for impartiality among those opposed to relocation of Centralia. They see it as a mouthpiece for the Concerned Citizens. . . . Unfortunately, the divided perceptions among the townspeople of the value of their local paper creates an additional impediment to unification of the town behind a solution: the largest accessible source of information is easily discounted by a large number. Intervention by an outside agent would require a careful aloofness from this little daily.[22]

After a disaster of natural origin, the print and electronic media provide information on where to go and what to do. While the extent of physical damage, human loss, and social disruption caused by the disaster agent are frequently subject to unrealistic reporting, media distortion is not a major factor in defining responses to the disaster. In a chronic technological disaster, on the other hand, residents are much less sure of what is happening to them and their community. The evidence of the hazard is ill-defined and contradictory; government response is marked by discontinuity and uncertainty. The case of Centralia suggests a relationship between the degree of uncertainty associated with an aversive agent and the likelihood that the media will expand their role of providing practical information into shaping perceptions and beliefs about the scope and seriousness of the hazard. It appears that the greater the perception of potential loss and the higher the degree of uncertainty, the more dependent a person or group becomes on the media's interpretation of a warning or threat cue. As we see it, the newspaper's one-sided orientation helped shape the beliefs of some residents about the fire and reinforced the opinions of others.

The threat beliefs that developed among the founding members of the CC centered on the perceived loss of ability to protect themselves and their children from toxic gases and mine cave-ins. They believed that their homes were no longer safe habitats; that parts of the community itself were now life-threatening; and that they had been abandoned by neighbors who did not understand or accept their interpretation of the crisis as life-threatening; and that the government would not, or could not, protect them.

The CC perceived a loss of control over essential areas of everyday life. The house, the yard, and the neighborhood were no longer predictable arenas in which to conduct the affairs of communal life. Moreover, this loss of control was not seen as a temporary inconvenience, to be corrected within a reasonable period of time. There would be no quick solution, given the technical difficulties in abating the fire and the inconsistent, politically motivated, seemingly conspiratorial response of government. The sociological message of the threat beliefs was that the members of the CC were victims, attached not to the community as a whole but to one another in the anticipation of imminent danger.[23]

Given the conflicting information as to the dangers of the fire, many Centralians on the hot side of town feared the worst. They began to confirm each other's fears. The irony is that the vagueness and uncertainty of a chronic technological disaster, the terror of anticipating the unknown, call out for firm beliefs to interpret the threat. But beliefs based on worst-case interpretations evoke stress responses that may ultimately be more damaging to the person and the community than the hazard agent itself; there need not be a close fit between the nature of a threat and the nature of the reaction. In other words, the meaning of a high gas reading or a subsidence resided not in the event itself but in the interpretation of the event. In a very real sense, the members of the CC were victimized twice: once by the mine fire, and once again by the chronic state of apprehension generated by their threat beliefs.

The fears arising from the group's beliefs pushed it to adopt what we will call confrontational coping from among the possible range of behaviors for preventing, avoiding, or controlling the sources of stress. In its confrontational tactics, the CC relied on emotional displays of anger to dramatize the danger and to confront others, both within and outside the town, with their moral responsibility toward the victims of the fire.[24]

This confrontational coping had both expressive and instrumental functions. On the one hand, it served as a safety valve for releasing a portion of the frustration and anger that members of the CC were feeling. On the other hand, confrontational coping can be seen as an emotional crusade to control the way in which neighbors and extra-local agencies and legislators interpreted the predicament. CC members, who wanted to be seen as victims of a disaster agent that was out of control, demanded swift and drastic action to reduce the immediate risks to health and safety. Other Centralians, however, feared that the CC might bring about destruction of the community itself. In the end, although the confrontational tactics did help to move the federal and state governments toward greater accountability in Centralia, they also alienated the CC from those in the community who viewed the fire's dangers as minimal and the CC's tactics, therefore, as self-serving and destructive. The nature of the controversy in Centralia shifted from disagreements over technical issues to rank antagonism, pitting those who sought to preserve the borough from what they perceived to be a controllable problem against those who demanded to be relieved from a chronic state of fear for their lives, even if it meant that Centralia had to be destroyed.

5. Confrontation and Conflict

We lived all our lives in Centralia;
It's here that our families have grown;
But fire's now threatening our city.
It's driving us out of our home.

The coal companies took all our riches;
Big money they made and amassed.
And now they left us in Centralia,
With nothing but poisonous gas.
                    —"Mine Fire Ballad," by a CC member

The Concerned Citizens Against the Centralia Mine Fire had an impact on the town that was completely out of proportion to its brief existence. In the twenty-one months from its first meeting, in March of 1981, until the officers of the organization resigned in November of 1982, the CC polarized the community. The mine fire itself took second place to the schisms between competing groups, displayed in anger and hostility and sustained by disagreements over specific issues associated with the fire.[1]

Many Centralians outside the CC were concerned about the fire and wanted to do something about it but could not accept the confrontational style of the CC. As one cold-side resident explained: "Do the CC think that they are the only ones that are concerned? I'm worried and so is my neighbor across the street. So are a lot of people. But yelling and pointing fingers is not going to solve the problem. But that's all they [CC] do as far as I can tell."

Through the tactics of confrontation, the group sought to impose on other Centralians its definition of the crisis, based on its ecologically specific experiences of the fire. The belief that group members were in extreme danger left them little choice but to confront their neighbors with the awful "truth" that Centralia was a perilous place to live. The CC did not want to alienate their neighbors, they wanted to warn them. Ironically, however, it was the group's confrontational style and not the content of their warning message that most Centralians responded to.

The CC's first public meeting sent a clear signal to many Centralians that, for the group, "doing something" about the fire outweighed any considerations of preserving the community. In late March 1981, after reading newspaper accounts of the formation of the group, an attorney from a nearby town contacted the president of the CC to bring up the possibility of litigation. The attorney offered to meet with the group to discuss strategies for bringing legal action against the government, forcing it to respond to those residents who were suffering the effects of the fire. In a move they would label naive months later, the group accepted the attorney's offer and decided to make their first meeting public, inviting anyone from the community to attend. At the meeting, on March 30 at Borough Hall, the attorney listed several options for litigation. In his view, the initial lawsuit would be brought against Centralia's Borough Council, the next one against the state, and the third against the federal government. Hearing that legal action against the Borough Council was proposed, the mayor of the borough stormed out of the meeting and called the other council members to tell them that this fledgling group was going to sue the borough. Word quickly spread through the small town.

Although the CC decided against pursuing the attorney's strategy and did not invite him back, the damage had been done. From the perspective of many in the borough, the CC members wanted to protect themselves even if it meant sacrificing the interests of the community. Not in a mood to placate its opponents, the CC made no effort to correct the community's misperception of its intentions. In fact, one councilman reported that for several months after the initial meeting, he had expected every day to receive notice that he was being sued.

Meanwhile, although deciding against litigation, the CC did not give up its confrontational coping strategy. On April 22, 1981, the group, now officially called the Concerned Citizens Against the Centralia Mine Fire, held its first meeting as a chartered organization. The meeting began with a discussion of what group members could do to alert the rest of the town, as well as government agencies and legislators, to their plight. "We wanted to do something that would make this community get off its duff and realize how serious this problem was," observed a former member of the group. With the sense of urgency that comes from living in a constant state of fear, the group decided to stage a protest march down the center of town, to dramatize their fears and convince others in town of the dangers they too were facing.

Although the protest was originally to take place on April 26, the group rescheduled it to May 12, when a community meeting would be held in the evening at the Borough Hall to discuss a nonbinding referendum on the fire. The CC's postponement of the protest gave the local paper time to report the CC's plans in advance. In its first news article on the organization, the daily reported that the "Concerned Citizens plan to stage a protest march just before the start of a public meeting May 12 on the May 19 referendum in the borough."[2]

This article led to several complaints from residents regarding the propriety of the march. An elderly man complained that "protests were for college kids. This is a quiet town. We don't need a riot here. It won't accomplish anything." His wife was equally opposed to the march: "It's embarrassing to have a few people running around with signs telling the world that my town isn't a safe place to live." The treasurer of the CC admitted to the reporter covering the story that he was "getting a lot of questions about the march. Some people don't like the idea."

In the late afternoon of May 12, twenty CC members met at the north end of town and marched south to Borough Hall. The marchers wore red ribbons on their clothing and tied ribbons to their porches and on telephone poles, to symbolize both the mine fire and the governmental red tape that had allowed the fire to continue for twenty years. Not wanting to overdramatize their situation, group members had decided to forgo wearing gas masks. The signs that the marchers carried proclaimed: "Ask not what your government can do for you, it doesn't give a damn"; "Watt [the U.S. Interior Secretary] is the problem in Centralia"; "Save our town! Put out the mine fire."

Several children and reporters were in the audience, but very few Centralians were on the streets to watch the marchers. Some people opened their curtains to catch a glimpse of the group as they passed, but many were already at the Borough Hall, waiting for the community meeting to begin. Contrary to the CC's expectations, the protest march did not dramatize its beliefs or impress on Centralia the need for action. Instead, the march called attention to the group's apparent disregard for the propriety of community life in Centralia. "That march was like a bunch of silly children trying to get their way," one woman objected. Another resident offered a more practical appraisal of the CC's march: "I understand their fears and I too would want to do something about my situation if I lived on the hill, but marching down the center of town like a bunch of crazies is not going to put the fire out."

Community disapproval of the march was expressed by more than name-calling. Many in town began avoiding the members of the organization. Neighbors crossed the street rather than encounter a member of the CC, and even long-standing friendships dissolved. CC leaders began receiving anonymous phone calls from muffled voices: "How can you be so goddamned stupid to spout off like that" or "Keep your mouth shut. There is no problem." As the months went by, the calls became more vicious, threatening bodily harm and even death.

Confronting the community, first with an attorney who recommended suing the Borough Council and then with a protest march down the center of town, the CC signaled loud and clear to many Centralians that its ties to its threat beliefs were stronger than its ties to the unity and identity of the borough. For most Centralians, however, the group's beliefs were not supported by sufficient evidence to warrant their displays. "If they are so sick from the gases," reasoned one man, "how come it is that they have all this energy for marching and meetings?"

Living in a state of chronic vigilance, CC members did not pursue a rational plan of organizing the community, and their emotion-driven strategies backfired. Although the group had hoped to mobilize the town around its beliefs, its initial attempts at emphasizing the harm done by the fire were interpreted by many as a rejection of the community. Seeking to convince their neighbors that Centralia was in imminent peril, CC members themselves began to be perceived by many Centralians as endangering the preservation of the town. Thus emerged what George Simmel has called the phenomenon of "social hatred."[3] The CC members viewed many of their neighbors as enemies who callously disregarded the dangers to which residents on the hill were exposed. In the view of many Centralians, however, CC members were traitors to the community, willing to sacrifice the borough for their own ends.

Both sides could find support for their positions in the endless parade of conflicting interpretations of the fire that came from various government agencies. During the second week in March 1981, the Office of Surface Mining publicly designated the area on the hill between Second Street and South Street as "most critical." About fifteen homes were within this area. A smaller plot adjacent to South Street was labeled "less critical." One CC member was able to find some humor in the latter classification: "Does less critical mean that I can be less careful than if I lived in the most critical area, but should be more careful than if I lived in a least critical area?" When asked what the designation meant in terms of protecting family members from harm, an OSM official responded predictably: "I am afraid that is an issue the state of Pennsylvania will have to address. This agency's responsibilities begin and end with the technical aspects of the problem."

With the official announcement of a "most critical" and a "less critical" area in the borough, we might expect that public perception of the extent and kind of danger from the fire would shift toward the threat beliefs of the CC. But within a few days of the OSM's official designation of danger areas, the typical pattern of contrary evidence emerged, ensuring that, like a Rorschach ink blot, the mine fire would be interpreted according to personal convictions rather than objective fact.

Several days after the official pronouncement of "most" and "less" critical sections of the community, the Roman Catholic Church assessed the safety of students in its parochial school, which was located adjacent to the "most critical" section. Easily visible from the school were the gaping ends of large pipes that vented carbon gases from the underground blaze. The school was monitored daily for the presence of carbon monoxide gas, and the DER had recorded levels of CO in excess of 35 parts per million in the school on nineteen separate occasions during January and February. (Anything above 10 ppm is considered dangerous by the Pennsylvania Department of Health. Thirty-five ppm is considered uninhabitable.) But a DER official was quick to point out that many of the high readings were related to such routine events as cooking in the school cafeteria, power surges in the electrical system, or smoking cigarettes. Concerned about the welfare of the children in the school, the bishop of the Harrisburg Diocese sent a representative to Centralia to assess the hazard and determine what should be done.

At the conclusion of his visit, the diocesan representative's evaluation was: "At this point I don't have any good reason to recommend closing the school." In paraphrasing the representative's remarks, the local paper wrote, "the Diocese of Harrisburg . . . indicated that occasional presence of carbon monoxide gas in the school in non-life-threatening amounts would be tolerated by the diocese."[4] Once again, this time in the form of official pronouncements from both state and church, residents of Centralia were presented with contrasting judgments of the scope and severity of the mine fire crisis. Many residents would interpret these official conclusions as mutually exclusive, focusing on one or the other as authorized proof of their particular definition of the problem.

Mirroring the confusion in March 1981 about what harm the fire might do, several families responded ambiguously to offers from the government for temporary housing. Five of the families most at risk from gas emissions and subsidence (four of them members of the CC) had asked the Pennsylvania Emergency Management Agency to provide house trailers for them to move into until a decision could be made about permanent relocation. The Pennsylvania Department of Health approved the families for trailers, citing the danger of subsidence, the threat of poisonous gases in the homes, and the medical histories of the family members as reasons for approval. The department's official certification of the potential for harm and the agency's recommendation for temporary relocation seemed to be a clear signal that several families were immediately at risk. Yet three of the five families rejected the government's offer to move into the trailers. One resident feared his family would become "forgotten people" in a trailer, like flood victims who accept interim housing.[5] Other families complained of the expense of maintaining two dwellings. Whatever their reasons, the refusal of some families to accept the government's offer was evidence for many Centralians that the problems the families had complained about were really not very serious. To quote one cold-sided resident: "Here the government comes along and says 'Okay, we're going to help you with your problem. Here are some trailers. Move in.' And what do these yellers and screamers do? Make excuses for not moving." Once again, confirmation of the fire's hazards was followed by discreditation in a cycle that defeated any possibility of community consensus.

On April 25, 1981, the local paper printed a story headlined "Fire Threat Is Minimized." The story quoted the deputy legal counsel to Governor Richard Thornburgh of Pennsylvania in describing the U.S. Department of the Interior's assessment of the fire: "They explained to us that they view the threat as one that

will dissipate, given the configuration of the coal seams and other
conditions of the fire." Later in the article, however, the writer
cited a contradictory report from the U.S. Bureau of Mines on
the consequences of allowing the fire to burn uninterrupted:
"This . . . would result in the fire's lasting many years. . . . Over
one-half of the borough of Centralia . . . could become involved
in the fire hazards. . . . It is clear that the 'do nothing' approach
would require relocating the entire community of Centralia."[6]

Even when one source of harm was ruled out, another replaced
it. The community was relieved to hear in June of 1981 that the
deadly gas methane had not been detected in a sewer trench
opened on the hot side of town;[7] perhaps the gases were not the
problem the CC claimed they were. A month later, however, a
representative of Nader's Public Interest Coalition formally requested the state Department of Health to test the air in Centralia homes for gases other than CO and methane, including
sulfur oxides and benzopyrene. The president of the CC said of
the request: "There's a lot more danger here than at Three Mile
Island."[8]

During the summer, Interior Secretary Watt and Governor
Thornburgh signed what was officially known as a memorandum
of understanding, which was to have clarified the roles that the
state and the OSM would play in finding a solution for Centralia.
This memo, however, was interpreted differently by the federal
and the state governments. The federal interpretation of the
memo reduced the OSM's responsibility in Centralia to carrying
out the planned purchase of twenty-seven houses in the impact
zone. According to the OSM, its responsibility in the Centralia
mine fire was finished upon completion of the buyout. As the
state executive office interpreted the memo, the OSM's active
role would continue until the crisis ended. The question of the
OSM's responsibility received it's full share of media attention
and became a source of anxiety for many Centralians who knew
that the state's resources were too limited to abate or extinguish
the fire. A memorandum, however, is not a legal document, and

the U.S. Congress ensured that the OSM continued to take the lead agency role in the Centralia crisis. The "Memorandum of Misunderstanding," as it was called in Centralia, faded from public concern, but not without seriously discrediting the image of Interior Secretary James Watt and his agency.

Even more significant than the memorandum in compromising the credibility of the OSM was the agency's purchase of twenty-seven homes in July and August. In 1980, when the OSM had purchased six properties on East Park Street, homeowners were satisfied that the OSM had appraised their properties fairly, and few complaints were voiced. In contrast, the buyout during the summer of 1981 aroused the ire of many Centralians, who complained vociferously. The owners of the twenty-seven properties, located in the most dangerous area of town, received appraisal figures for their homes and then had ten days to decide whether or not to accept the government's offer. The homeowners, other residents, and local officials assumed that the prices offered would be calculated in the same manner as the 1980 appraisals, which took no account of the mine fire. Almost everyone was surprised and dismayed to learn that the twenty-seven families eligible for relocation would lose an average of 20 percent in the appraised value of their homes because of the mine fire. The OSM justified its change in appraisal policy by citing the 1977 Surface Mining Control and Reclamation Act, but few people were satisfied with this argument since the legislation had not been a factor in the 1980 buyout. An OSM lawyer had warned the Department of the Interior several months before the 1981 buyout that it was debatable whether or not mine fires fell within the jurisdiction of the 1977 law.[9]

Amidst all this confusion, the fledgling CC was having little success. When strategies to win community support had quite the opposite effect, the CC spent less time in trying to elicit community support and more time in writing to newspapers and government officials. The group also turned to social service agencies for assistance. Although the CC had not been successful in organizing the community around its threat beliefs, writing letters to the press and government agencies was an effective means of affirming these beliefs. Unable to control the community's interpretation of the crisis, the group began to write emotional, frequently accusatory letters to elected officials, emphasizing their moral obligation to support and assist a community that lived in a constant state of dread. Through their letters, group members found ready allies in environmental and community action agencies ready to affirm and intensify the worst-case interpretation of the crisis.

On May 5, 1981, the CC wrote to the editors of eleven newspapers and five months later to more than a dozen newspapers. A steady stream of correspondence was also directed at government officials. Indeed, one member of the group admitted to getting quite tired of typing letter after letter, particularly since very few were answered. Despite the lack of response, the letters provided a means for the group to ratify its interpretation of the crisis by giving it permanence through the written word.[10] Just as neighbors turned away from this hostile group, however, so did most upper echelon officials of government agencies (though for different reasons).

On April 26, 1981, the CC sent its first letter to Governor Thornburgh. The purpose of this and other letters to officials was not to ask for specific, practical assistance. Instead, the letters were intended to convince the officials of their moral accountability to the town for relief from the fire. The following are excerpts from the April 26 letter.

As President of the Concerned Citizens Action Group Against the Centralia Mine Fire . . . I am most anxious . . . over the news that the Department of the Interior . . . is abandoning the Centralia Mine Fire Project. I cannot strongly enough protest such action, particularly since toxic gases from the mine fire are becoming more and more prevalent. . . . When someone dies from these toxic gases it is going to be too late, and the Government expressing sympathy and regret will fall on bitter ears . . . It seems to me that OSM's decision to pull out . . . smells of some sort of conspiracy on the part of the Government and because I feel this way, I must ask for, no, demand an investigation.[11]

Copies of this letter were sent to two U.S. senators, President Ronald Reagan, Interior Secretary Watt, and others. Other letters to President Reagan, Watt, and several minor officials were also couched in the emotional language of the CC's threat beliefs.

A letter to the president of the United States from the president of the CC read:

I live in . . . Centralia Pennsylvania, a community that has watched a bad dream grow into a horrible nightmare. The nightmare . . . is an underground mine fire that has been raging for nineteen years. . . .

Dangerous . . . gases emitted by . . . the fire are seeping into homes endangering the lives of the people who live there. . . . Please help Centralia slay its . . . fire breathing dragon before [it] claims the life of even one innocent person."[12]

In their first letter to Watt, CC members threw down the gauntlet:

We have written asking what is to be done about the fire and are told that [the] situation is being closely watched and that the problem has been temporarily solved by the acquisition of a 16 acre area. Hogwash! . . . More and more homes outside the 16 acre area are having problems with gases, both Carbon Monoxide and Carbon Dioxide, the latter of which, in some cases, is creating dangerously low oxygen problems endangering people's lives. . . . Because our lives have been greatly endangered by this fire, I am compelled to ask must people here die like people in Carbondale, Pa. died from their mine fire before positive action is taken."[13]

As we argued earlier, guided by the democratic ethos of representation and the more practical need for the vote, legislators were generally supportive of the group. Indeed, on more than one occasion, an elected official felt the need to document his concern for the crisis by relating his activities on behalf of the community: "Since I took office on January 5, 1981, my staff and I have spent an average of 20 to 30 hours per week on the problem in Centralia. It has my utmost attention."[14]

More than simply verifying their concern, however, legislators had the propensity to accuse, blame, and generally malign various technical agencies at the state and federal levels. The CC was a receptive audience for lawmakers frustrated in their attempts to champion a cause that was receiving national attention.

In one letter to the group, a member of the state House of Representatives accused the Pennsylvania Emergency Management Agency (PEMA) and the governor of failing to disclose a critical document. At the request of the governor, PEMA had conducted and turned over to the governor's office a study assessing the real dangers of the fire. Subsequent efforts to have the document released to the public were stonewalled by the state executive office. The state legislator wrote to the hyper-vigilant CC: "Please be advised that I have attempted to obtain a copy of the 16 page report of the Pennsylvania Emergency Management Agency to Governor Thornburgh, regarding the Centralia Mine Fire." The Governor's office, he continued, "refused to turn over the Report and added that at this time there are no plans to *ever* make that Report public. . . . I can't tell you how upsetting the Federal and State Administrations' attitude disturbs me [sic]. Centralia is being treated as a pawn in a cruel chess game. No one wants to pay the fiddler, only pass the buck."[15]

Buck-passing was an experience with which CC members were too familiar, as the following letter to them from a deputy director of the Bureau of Mines illustrates: "We have been requested by the Assistant Secretary for Fossil Energy of the Department of Energy to respond to your letter . . . to that agency. . . . On February 1, 1982, the Secretary of the Interior transferred mine land demonstration and reclamation projects conducted by the Bureau of Mines to the Office of Surface Mining. Since this transfer includes all bureau activities relating to the Centralia mine fire, we are taking the liberty of referring your letter to OSM. . . . If we can be of any further assistance, please let us know."[16] OSM did not respond to the CC letter.

Doing nothing for the image of the OSM, a U.S. congressman wrote the CC complaining of the recalcitrant behavior of this federal agency: "It is most frustrating that even when the Congress provides the Department with clear directions for use of these funds, OSM still fails to develop a plan to provide some meaningful assistance in addressing the mine fire problem."[17]

In view of letters like these, CC members came to regard themselves as victims of infighting between legislators and government agencies. Their confidence in the capacity or the willingness of extra-local government to bring the fire under control continued to erode in the face of letters from key legislators openly accusing executive agencies and officials of cover-ups, negligence, and dilatory behavior. Indeed, in one particularly inflamatory letter, a state representative advocated that "the United States Congress cite Secretary James Watt for contempt."[18]

Technical agencies, quite independent of the lawmakers, wrote letters that did little more than intensify the highly charged emotions of fear and anger among the group. A common tactic of the Department of the Interior was to respond to inquiries by sending the same letter or portions of the same letter to different members of the CC. Several portions of a June 22, 1981, letter to a young married couple active in the CC reappeared in a July 14 response to an inquiry by the president of the CC. In this case, both letters were signed by the same OSM official. The group was even more incensed when it received identical letters, sent within three weeks of one another, from two different OSM officials. "They [the OSM] must have a form letter," observed one CC member, "that they just pull out of a file and mail. Sincere, aren't they!"

On more than one occasion, representatives of the governor's office wrote to CC members to chide them for their confrontational posture, as in a letter from Thornburgh's deputy general counsel: "A positive attitude on the part of all concerned would seem to be particularly appropriate under these circumstances."[19] At least one member expressed the feeling of entrapment: "Here we sit. Caught between our town who doesn't care and our Governor who cares about only one thing, his political future."

Certain passages from letters were read aloud and reread during CC meetings, giving the group ample time to interpret their meaning according to the logic of the threat beliefs. For example, on August 11, 1981, the group received a letter from the Interior Department's assistant director of abandoned mine lands: "OSM will continue, as it has in the past, to make all reasonable efforts to protect the health and safety of the people living in the fire area."[20] In group discussion, the phrase "as it has in the past" took on a meaning quite different from that presumably intended by the assistant director. "If they continue as they have in the past," commented a Concerned Citizen, "this fire will burn forever." In addition, the group found quite inappropriate the use of the word "reasonable." When the stakes are health and even life itself, they mused, should the efforts be limited only to those considered "reasonable"?

All in all, the CC sent more than eighty letters between March 1981 and November 1982, and received more than fifty letters in response.[21] This correspondence was a major means of maintaining the threat belief system that had been created to reduce the anxiety of uncertainty. Far from alleviating the CC's fears, the pattern of the letters responding to the group's inquiries served to confirm their worst-case interpretations. Commiserated with by legislators, patronized by technical agencies, and admonished by the governor's office, the group grew in political acumen as it witnessed the incapacity at all levels of government to act decisively on Centralia's behalf.

The operations of the CC were isolated from the community's influence. The group met regularly in public as well as private sessions, but nonmembers rarely attended the public meetings. Indeed, most Centralians avoided CC members and their activities entirely, leaving no opportunity for the expression and resolution of conflicting beliefs about the fire. In an open demonstration of the town's opinion of the CC, the Centralia Borough Council eventually prevented the group from holding its formal sessions in Borough Hall, claiming that the CC was a disruptive influence in the town. Their enforced separation from community life made CC members even more dependent on group meetings, where they reinforced their threat beliefs and reaffirmed their differences from their neighbors. As the group failed to legitimate itself in the public life of the village, its public meetings became fewer and its private meetings more frequent. Early in the group's career, public meetings were held once a week, but then lapsed to twice a month, and in the last several months of the CC's existence, to only once a month.

The structure of both public and private CC gatherings was much the same: both emphasized the sharing of fears and the expression of anger. A typical formal meeting opened in the routine way for a business meeting, with a financial report from the treasurer and a review of the minutes of the previous gathering. Various officers then read aloud letters received or to be sent, which frequently accounted for as much as thirty minutes per meeting. When the president opened the way for contributions from the floor, the meeting would almost invariably break down into a cacophony of voices, as the following field note illustrates:

After reading several letters, the president opened the meeting, looking at the group and saying, 'Well what's on your mind tonight?' That question triggered a series of seemingly random statements by several people: "I'm worried that we are losing steam. I guess we need another subsidence to put a spark under everyone." Another person responded with, "Regardless of what happens the townsfolk will find a way not to believe it." "They all stand behind their curtains," observed another person, "watching what's going on."

Seeking to bring the discussion around to something useful, the Vice-President asked, "Does anybody have any suggestions?" "How about selling bumper stickers?," suggested one woman. "I wonder if it's safe to go in my backyard," responded another woman to no one in particular. . . . These disconnected expressions continued for over twenty minutes.

The social isolation of the CC ensured that no alternative interpretations of the crisis would be introduced into its meetings for consideration by the group. Without any voice to speak for a less dreadful, more manageable perspective on the crisis, CC meetings became occasions for reinforcement of personal fears, disbelief in neighbors' ability or willingness to appreciate the dangers of the fire, and generalized anger toward a world that could no longer protect the CC members: "There are people in this town who would see us die before they admitted that there's a problem. . . . I mean can you believe it? There are rumors that CC planned to have——fall in that subsidence to get attention! Now, how can you fight that ignorance?"

The security of the group encouraged expressions of the heart, not the mind; of passionate feelings, not deliberate, reflective thought. In short, the CC's meetings did not function to reduce the emotive means of coping, but to intensify it.

The CC found no ally in local government. CC members saw the Borough Council as representing primarily the residents of the cold side of town. In trying to fulfill its mandated role of representing the will of all Centralians, the Borough Council provided the arena in which the different factions met to do verbal battle. Often turning into emotionally charged shouting matches, Borough Council meetings were the most visible symbol of the divisiveness that wracked the town, attesting to the above-ground disaster that was destroying the social community.

Beyond providing the stage for conflict, the Borough Council's role in the mine fire was relatively limited: it sponsored two referenda on mine fire issues, became the liaison between state and federal agencies and community residents, and would oc-

casionally go on record as favoring a certain course of action. But
by and large, the Borough Council failed to take a strong leadership role, creating a vacuum that the CC attempted to fill.

The fact that the Borough Council failed to provide effective
leadership throughout this prolonged crisis is not surprising,
given the nature and structure of Centralia's government.[22] The
borough is governed by a system that strictly limits the mayor's
authority and gives the bulk of what executive power there is to
the council. Composed of citizens who volunteer their time and
effort, the Borough Council's functions are clearly custodial during normal times. Untrained volunteer leadership may be sufficient for taking care of the everyday business of a small
municipality. But when confronted with a crisis that jeopardized
the community's health and safety, indeed its very existence,
this form of local government could not be expected to respond
effectively to the myriad demands.

Indeed, as the mine fire burned on, few citizens were willing
to take on formal leadership roles. At the reorganization meeting
of January 7, 1980, over a year before the CC was organized,
four new Borough Council members were sworn in, but nobody
was willing to take on the responsibility of council president. It
was not until the fourth nomination that a new councilman re-
luctantly agreed to serve. At the June 2 meeting, to improve the
handling of information, the Borough Council designated its
president as the liaison with other government agencies—against
the president's will; his was the only "no" vote on the motion.

Throughout 1980, mine fire issues for the council were largely
of an informational nature. A representative of the Bureau of
Mines regularly presented a report on the status of a drilling
project that was gathering information as the basis for an OSM
decision about the fire. At times, the council expressed frustration that no representative with authority (from the OSM) was
present to answer questions about possible options.[23]

The few other matters that came before the council seem to
have been handled with dispatch. Council members forcefully
protested attempts by the county to divert federal Housing and

Urban Development money from use in Centralia.[24] They also expressed concern about Centralians' safety. When two residents who attended the August 4 meeting stated that a Bureau of Mines official had told them they were living "in a mine atmosphere" because of the influx of gases in their home, the council wrote to the OSM insisting that something be done to guarantee the safety of this family.

At the same time, there is no evidence from the minutes of its meetings that the council exercised any leadership role in the mine fire crisis; given the history of the borough and the custodial nature of council, this would have been expecting too much. And yet the absence of forceful local leadership would have critical consequences during the first half of 1981.

The Borough Council clearly failed to act forcefully in response to one of the more critical events in the Centralia story, the narrow escape of the twelve-year-old boy from a subsidence on February 14, 1981. The only mention of the subsidence in the minutes of the council's March 2 meeting was made in reference to the continuing presence of gas in the area. It was in reaction to the boy's near-tragedy that the CC was formed. One can only speculate that had the Borough Council taken decisive action at this point, the formation of the CC might not have been necessary. At the same council meeting, in response to a suggestion by the U.S. congressman for Centralia's district, a motion was passed to ask Columbia County to place a referendum on the May primary election ballot asking Centralians: "Do you favor Excavation & Relocation of the entire Community as a solution to the present Mine Fire and/or dangers created by the Mine Fire?"[25] In a letter accompanying the motion, a councilman stated: "This referendum is direly needed by the Council so that it . . . can act according to the will of the majority of its Citizens. I make this motion because I feel that Council should not have such a heavy and unfair burden placed on its shoulders."[26]

The proposal to hold a referendum was one of the few occasions when the Borough Council and the CC agreed on a course of action, and when the vote was held the fledgling CC lobbied their neighbors to get out and vote. But the interpretation of the vote was open to debate. On the surface, it appeared that a "yes" vote would indicate that the voter favored digging the fire out and relocating the community. Yet differing interpretations abounded. Even the author of the referendum motion stated that it did not really mean what it said: "Councilman . . . said a 'yes' vote means a voter wants the federal government to come up with a just and workable solution to the mine fire. He said a 'yes' vote does not mean a voter favors only total excavation of the mine fire or complete relocation of Centralia."[27]

In the end, the referendum carried, with a two-to-one majority voting "yes." The CC interpreted this as a solid vote for relocation. But the Borough Council decided that the vote meant Centralians favored an engineering solution to the fire—total excavation—and not relocation, a solution that might mean the end of the town. At its July 6 meeting, the council moved that a resolution be sent to the Secretary of the Interior stating that the council favored total excavation as a solution to the fire. The resolution did not mention relocation.

Before the council could follow up on its resolution, however, a newly elected council took office. The new council was even more reluctant than the old one to take any position that might jeopardize the continued existence of the borough. The first official indication came at the November 2 meeting, when "Council went on record as being opposed to having———serve as liaison for Centralia with the Mine Fire Task Force. As early as 1969———was known to be a strong force behind relocation movement in Centralia." Apparently, the referendum results did not govern this council's view of what should be done about the fire. Indeed, at the November 2 meeting, the council "went on record to make a decision concerning the mine fire after the borehole project is completed and results are known."

The decision by the new council to disregard the referendum results and wait for additional research before taking action angered the CC. Members of the CC attended council meetings and vociferously demanded that the council force the state and federal governments to take immediate action to protect health and safety, even to the point of relocating the borough. The council would respond that action that could destroy the borough was unnecessary and rash; moreover, council members resented the CC's attempts to take over decision making for the borough.

Unable to win the Borough Council over and lacking the resources and expertise to organize the community alone, the CC looked to outsiders, finding allies in various social service agencies. In reaching outside the community, CC members continued Centralia's historical pattern of external management of internal community affairs. Commenting in retrospect, an officer of the CC explained why the group sought leadership from organizations outside the community: "Let's face it, what did we know about community organizing? We were just a bunch of people who said 'Hey, we've got a problem' . . . and we were glad, I think, for any help we could get."

During April of 1981, the CC sought assistance from Ralph Nader's Center for Responsive Law. Several days later, a Nader representative and a member of the Washington, D.C.–based Energy Action Group visited Centralia to meet with the CC. The two met exclusively with group members; no effort was made to talk with others in town. In fact, the CC purposely changed the meeting location at the last minute because of rumors that several townspeople were going "to crash it and cause trouble." The CC's concluding minutes of the meeting note: "If we send all information—they will read same and possibly investigate on a Federal Level—representatives were very optimistic in our favor."[28]

The Nader agency assigned a toxicologist to examine data on the amount and kind of gases to which residents were exposed. At one point the toxicologist recommended that the DER test for a wider range of gases than CO and methane. Aside from the limited assistance of the Nader scientist, however, the CC received no further support from either the Center For Responsive Law or the Energy Action Group.

By June, only three months after the group had organized, morale was already low. Attendance at meetings was falling off. Letter writing "in the hope of getting some action from the officials" was too limited an activity to engage the group as a whole. It was now clear that the referendum, with its unequivocal message that a majority of the town wanted relief from the fire, was not a vote in favor of the CC. By this time it had become painfully clear to group members that their neighbors were not willing to support them. Indeed, friends and acquaintances had banished them, as if they and not the fire were the problem. Commenting in retrospect on the community anger directed toward the CC, one of its founders said, "We knew we were going to be a minority group."

In this period of growing despair, a representative of Rural American Women (RAW) called the vice-president of the CC,[29] asking for an invitation to Centralia to talk with the group about their predicament. At this point, the group was embracing any sign of support, and a meeting was scheduled to hear what this community organizer had to offer.

Like other social activist agencies, the RAW would visit a community only if invited by a local group. This policy is similar to the standard practice of clinical psychologists who, with few exceptions, work only with people who voluntarily submit for counseling or therapy. The principle is simply that personal or collective change is accomplished only when the person or group desires change. In the case of social agencies, an invitation from a host group is the first step in mobilizing a town.

As did Nader's Center for Responsive Law and the Energy Action Group, the RAW worked exclusively with the Concerned Citizens, their host group. It was the CC that drew the RAW's attention to Centralia, and it was the CC's threat beliefs that structured the RAW's interpretation of the crisis. From the beginning, the RAW accepted without question the worst-case interpretation of the crisis, an approach typical of social activist organizations, which routinely base their organizing strategies on the host group's definition of the crisis. The activities of the social activists are initially directed toward assisting the host group to become an effective organizing agent. The implicit assumption behind this strategy is that the host group represents, or has the potential to represent, the community.

The following, from a pamphlet distributed by the RAW, "Why we are involved in Centralia," illustrates the typical host group strategy: "We are involved with the citizens of Centralia, Pennsylvania—the Concerned Citizen's Action Group Against the Centralia Mine Fire—because they asked RAW to assist them in their organizing efforts. We felt we had the capabilities to do this, and believed the citizens had done the major work of mobilizing local people to assume some responsibility for the future of their community. . . . We work in communities where there is the reality of community togetherness."[30]

This description of Centralia citizens as organized and embodying "the reality of community togetherness" is clearly distorted. What is described in this passage is the RAW's ideal model of grassroots action, not the reality of what was going on in Centralia. Ironically, far from serving the ideal functions of a host group, the CC, renegades in Centralia, ensured that any agency linked to the group would be prevented from gaining access to the community. Throughout its time in Centralia, the RAW would remain identified with the CC, considered by many Centralians to be part of the problem.

Almost immediately after entering Centralia, the RAW intensified the already antagonistic relationship between the CC and the Borough Council. On the basis of one informal meeting with several councilmen, the RAW reported to the CC that local government "was afraid to act" and would be a "stumbling block" to the efforts of the group to achieve its aims. Corresponding to the CC's view of local government, this information justified the group's anger toward the council.

By late July 1981, the RAW was sending a representative from Washington to attend the CC's biweekly meetings. The RAW sought funding for the group and was successful in securing several small grants to subsidize its activities. Using its extensive

network of social activist organizations, the RAW also encouraged
CC members to contact several environmental action groups to
express concern over the dangers of exposure to mine fire gases.
Over several months, the CC received responses from various
environmental organizations, several of them confirmed the CC's
worst-case interpretation of the fire. In a letter from the director
of the organization, Appalachia–Science in the Public Interest,
CC members were urged to "accept my recommendation that
your town be monitored for sulfur oxides and other pollu-
tants. . . . You are close enough to Donora where an inversion
caused a number of pollution-related deaths back over a decade
ago."[31]

In a similar reply to the CC, the executive director of the
Delaware Valley Citizens' Council for Clean Air wrote: "I read
your letter and background information on the gases from the
Centralia fire. There is little doubt in my mind that sulfur dioxide
is being emitted by that fire, and the levels of SO_2 may pose a
serious health threat to the community."[32]

Despite the executive director's warning, at no time was SO_2
detected in more than normal rates in the impact zone. But more
significant than the warning is the closed information loop im-
plied in this excerpt. At the request of the RAW, the CC had
sent the initial letter explaining the CC's perception of the dangers of the fire, along with data attesting to the truth of its claims.
In replying with an honest appraisal of the only first-hand information it had received about the fire, the Council for Clean Air,
in turn, affirmed the CC's worst fears. The RAW thus assured
the CC of a sympathetic audience, but ironically, the more cor-
roboration the group received from sources remote from the
borough, the more intense the conflict became with it neighbors
within the borough.

After attending several CC meetings, it must have become
clear to the field organizers, irrespective of their public relations
pamphlet, that the CC's confrontational coping was doing little
more than alienating its neighbors. Nevertheless, the RAW pursued its normative model of community organizing, suggesting

to the CC that it sponsor two community trips, the first to Washington and the second to Harrisburg. The purpose of the trips was twofold: to lobby for an $850,000 borehole project that would at last determine the parameters of the fire, and to create two collective occasions in which everyone in town could participate. The Washington and Harrisburg trips would establish the CC as a serious group with concrete goals.

The RAW encouraged the CC to create a high profile in the weeks before the Washington trip. Media exposure was promoted. *PM Magazine* and several major newspapers, including the *New York Times,* the *Baltimore Sun,* and the *Washington Post,* were given exclusive stories, restricted to the CC's perceptions of the fire. As another way to publicize the CC and raise money for the Washington trip, the RAW suggested selling bumper stickers. After a spirited discussion, the CC decided that the bumper stickers, selling for a dollar apiece, would best express the feelings of the group if worded "Centralia, Pa. Mine Fire— HELL ON EARTH." The phrase caught the attention of many residents, but not with the results intended. "It's a crime that they [the CC] should be allowed to call our town a 'hell on earth,' " commented one woman. "If there's any hell in this town, it's the doings of CC that's causing it." In preparation for the Washington trip, the RAW issued a news release that opened with an expression of the CC's threat beliefs. " 'Listen,' says Ms.———, standing by that hole, 'you can hear the fires roaring.' For over 20 years, the fires have been burning near Centralia. . . . Now the fires have caught up with the people. The presence of hazardous gases in the homes and the cave-ins of the earth have already caused 31 families to move. . . . The Concerned Citizen's Action Group Against the Centralia Mine Fire will travel to Washington . . . October 19 and 20 to work toward resolution of this problem plaguing their community."[33]

Counseled by the RAW to use the Washington, D.C., journey as a basis for a "new spirit of cooperation" between the CC and the borough, the CC attended a Borough Council meeting to urge community residents and members of council to accompany the group to Washington. But CC members couched their appeal in a confrontational style. In fact, as the following quote from an officer of the CC indicates, the group fully expected to fail in its efforts to engender a "new spirit of cooperation": "It would be nice if a crowd went down to Washington just to show the federal government that we care about the problem. The trouble is, not enough people in Centralia care." The local press, reporting on the council meeting, captured the style of the CC appeal: "Members of CC lamented the lack of unity in the community and some townspeople's apathy about the mine fire." The council president, himself a member of the CC (but a cold-side resident), admonished the CC: "You have to appreciate other people's values. People are entitled to their own opinions. You should respect them."[34]

The fact is that most Centralians saw the Washington trip as a CC event, not a community effort. In the end, only six Centralians, all of them CC members, went on the bus to Washington—outnumbered by social service personnel who made the trip. Nonetheless, the CC viewed the mission as a success, if for no other reason than that it went beyond letter writing and emotional displays.

The RAW planned the group's two-day stay in the capital hour by hour, making sure those in attendance made the best use of their time. The itinerary planned by the RAW for October 14 and 15 included lunch with a law firm interested in representing beleaguered communities against big government, meetings with legislators from Pennsylvania and one from New York, and a meeting with an undersecretary for the Department of the Interior.

What is important for us about this trip is the dependence of the CC on the RAW for suggesting, organizing, and carrying out this activity. From the time of the RAW's initial involvement with the group early in the summer of 1981, it had steadily increased its directive role. Not surprisingly, the more direction the RAW provided the CC, the more dependent the group became on this social agency. Given the RAW's normative model of community organizing, it is reasonable to assume that had the CC constructed a solid base of community support, the RAW would have tapered off its participation. But the distance between the CC and the rest of Centralia's residents only lengthened with time, in part, ironically, because of the RAW's very involvement. The RAW's presence in Centralia and its advocacy role for the CC legitimated the threat beliefs of the CC. With most of their neighbors unsympathetic to their beliefs about the dangers of the fire, CC members grew dependent on the RAW and other agencies for assurances that their fears and anger were plausible.

Several days after the Washington trip, the efforts of the CC to persuade the community that its threat beliefs were plausible suffered a major setback when the newly appointed chief of the Division of Environmental Health in the Pennsylvania Department of Health publicly announced that the Centralia mine fire had never posed health and safety problems for the town's residents. It is not known what sources Dr. James Fox used to reach his conclusion. Repeated calls to the health department by both the CC and the press went unanswered. What is known is that conclusive evidence on the extent and severity of the fire awaited the data from the federal borehole project, which were released in the summer of 1983, almost two years after Dr. Fox's statement. The borehole data would discredit Fox's statement, but meanwhile his official pronouncement backed up those in Centralia who were predisposed to discredit the CC.

Even at the time of Fox's official declaration in October 1981 that the fire was not a threat, there was contradictory evidence. A few days before Fox's statement, one family in Centralia woke to the sound of their gas monitor, warning them that the CO level in their home had exceeded 35 parts per million. The children were removed from the home, and windows and doors were opened to permit the gas to escape. Word of this incident spread quickly among neighboring families. The day before the CC traveled to Washington, a car had almost been swallowed up by a subsidence, which left a gaping hole 8 by 12 feet. At the time, the car was being loaded with the household goods of a family forced to relocate because of the fire.

Both of these families must have been surprised in November at the local newspaper's bold headline "Watt believes mine fire safe."[35] As he was boarding a plane in New Orleans, Interior Secretary Watt had been overhead remarking that the Centralia mine fire posed "no threat to health and safety." Although Watt's public relations staff would try to modify his ill-timed assessment, arguing that what he really meant was that the fire was not a threat to everybody living in Centralia,[36] here was another piece of official intelligence for those who could not accept the threat beliefs of the CC.

Many Centralians, however, needed no official confirmation of their perceptions that the fire had only remote risks. In the words of one woman living on the hill, as reported by the paper on the day before Watt's statement: "Why would we give up our home? . . . We have freedom of choice. And we choose to stay. We do not feel we are in any danger . . . and we will be adamant in our position." "She believes," the paper continued, "that many things besides carbon monoxide from the mine fire are causing monitors to show the presence of carbon monoxide. She suggested that cigarette smoking . . . hair spray, cooking odors from sauerkraut or brussels sprouts, kerosene stoves and stove gas jets left on caused many of the gas readings."[37]

Against the jumble of official reports, personal experiences, and residents' perceptions, the CC planned its trip to Harrisburg, under the guidance of Catholic Social Services (CSS). On several occasions from early summer to November 1981, a CSS representative had accompanied the RAW spokesperson to CC meetings, and the task of managing the CC was gradually transferred. After the trip to Harrisburg, it was clear that the CC had shifted its dependence on the RAW to CSS. In her account of the RAW's withdrawal, a spokeswoman admitted that the seeming unwillingness of the town "to follow the lead of the CC" was causing RAW to reconsider its involvement in Centralia.

Catholic Social Services is a regionally based human service organization serving fifteen counties within the Harrisburg Diocese. Similar to RAW, CSS has as its primary mission to "organize and empower groups to become their own advocates for social change,"[38] and it too relies on the host group strategy. Like the RAW, CSS viewed the CC as the first block in building a communitywide organization, but its results were equally disappointing. The hostility that followed the CSS efforts to work through the CC culminated in death threats, slashed tires, and a fire bombing.

The first CC venture in which Catholic Social Services played the lead role, the Harrisburg trip, was widely advertised, but only nineteen CC members showed up and once again the Borough Council declined to accompany them.

CC members, who had been relatively composed in Washington, were emotional in their behavior and speech in Harrisburg. Among the comments directed at Pennsylvania officials: "We're asking for the truth, not half-truths and half-falsehoods"; "Why should we give up our lives to get help for Centralia?"; "This is unbelievable. How can you sit back and do nothing?" In an apparent effort at appeasement—the full meaning of which can only be appreciated against the backdrop of the official statements made by Watt and Fox several days earlier—the deputy counsel for Governor Thornburgh called the mine fire "an unprecedented disaster" comparable in magnitude and seriousness to the accident at Three Mile Island's nuclear plant. The CC returned from Harrisburg more convinced than ever that its worst-case interpretation of the crisis was indisputable.[39]

On their return from Harrisburg, fortified by contact with state officials, CC members lashed out at neighbors and local government for their apparent lack of concern. More and more frequently, in making judgments about responsibility for their misfortune, the CC pointed to the apathy of others in town. In time, CC members came to believe that they were victims as much of their neighbors' indifference as of the fire. Indeed, it is fair to say that the group was so preoccupied with the emotions

of fear and anger that the precipitating cause of the emotion, the
fire, became subordinate to the states of emotional arousal.

Driven by their threat beliefs, CC members were unable to
manage the emotional consequences of their fears. One irate
resident said of the CC's tactics: "Certain individuals in the community . . . make others suffer terribly, to the limit." Former
friends and acquaintances blamed the group for disrupting their
way of life. In the face of hostility or indifference, CC members
shifted from trying to recruit their neighbors to blaming them
for their calamity. In the months to come, as other grassroots
groups emerged, reciprocal blaming would characterize the
town's response to its crisis.

At this juncture in the history of the fire, the only organized
group at which CC members could direct their volatile emotions
was the Borough Council. Indeed, at first glance this elected
body was quite a likely target, being immediately responsible
for the welfare of the borough. Well placed to push for a solution
to the fire, the Borough Council was vulnerable to the CC's
charge of failing to assume a leadership role. As the year 1982
began, the council elected its third president in two years.[40] At
the first meeting of the reorganized council, arguments arose
over the new president's desire to dispense with the reading of
the minutes, and over the manner in which the borough solicitor
was appointed. These disagreements were only a prelude to the
dissension that would characterize the council meetings over the
next year and a half.

The 1982 council supported the federal government's $816,000
borehole project to delimit the fire, although the Borough Council had been wary from the beginning of its possible outcome.
Not trusting the impartiality of the forthcoming analysis of the
data by a federal consultant, the council discussed hiring an
independent engineer to evaluate the data. As early as March,
members of the Concerned Citizens were pushing the council
to take a stand on what should be done after the borehole project
was completed. With the encouragement of the CC, the council
had earlier drafted a letter to Interior Secretary Watt, urging

approval of the borehole project and periodic public reporting of borehole data. But beyond that, the council avoided taking a position, insisting that it must wait until the project was completed and the data studied.[41]

In anticipation that the borehole project would lead to a final solution, the level of community activity accelerated dramatically. Beginning in March, the council scheduled a second monthly meeting, which would deal exclusively with mine fire matters.[42] Throughout the spring and summer, a tremendous amount of information flowed through the council; correspondence was voluminous, and government officials appeared at council meetings to explain what was going to happen.

Much—perhaps too much—was expected of the council as the intermediary for communication between the federal and state governments and the community. In April, the council secretary put a memo on file stating that since assuming office, the new president had not been routing correspondence and other business records to her. In obvious frustration, she stated, "I cannot be held accountable for maintaining files when I am not given the documents to maintain as required by the Borough Code."[43]

Criticism of the council for the lack of communication was widespread, usually directed at the president. It was impossible to know objectively where the "blame" should lie. It was clear, however, that Centralians were focusing on the personalities of members of the various factions in fighting for their own perceived interests. This personalizing of the issues led to the development of much hostility and bitterness toward individual members of the community and did much to ensure that reconciliation between the different factions and groups would be impossible.

After accompanying the CC on the Harrisburg trip, Catholic Social Services sought money to subsidize the CC from the Campaign For Human Development, a granting agency within the United States Catholic Conference. Although CSS personnel were certainly aware that there was antagonism between the group and the rest of the community, they apparently did not know just how hostile the CC's relationship with the town had become. It is reasonable to assume that had CSS been aware of the extent and severity of the conflict among the townspeople, it would not have sought the funding. It was in the best interest of CSS to secure such a grant, because helping to address the celebrated problem in Centralia, where the greater part of the residents were Catholic, would indicate clearly the effectiveness of this social agency.

The grant was yet another idea that did not originate within the CC but with a social agency outside the community. It was CSS personnel who arranged meetings between the CC's officers and representatives of the Campaign for Human Development. It was, admits the officers of the CC, CSS grant writers who actually wrote the proposal. As in the other two major projects of the CC, the trips to Washington and Harrisburg, plans were made and goals accomplished not by CC members but by social service professionals.

In September 1982, the campaign for Human Development announced that it had awarded the CC a grant of $30,000, which surprised the group and horrified many Centralians. Working in isolation from the rest of town, the CC had informed few people outside the group about the grant proposal. Community reaction to the grant itself was swift and hostile. "What would possess anybody to give this group that wants to destroy our town money. . . . Can you believe it?" Letters from Centralians started pouring in to the diocesan bishop's office, protesting the grant, and several church members threatened to cancel their yearly pledge. Within days of the announcement, several CC members were harrassed by telephone calls, many of which threatened their lives. In telephoned death threats repeated over several weeks, a muffled voice would chant the phrase "You will not live to spend a penny of this money," then hang up. Ethno-religious prejudices revived. One woman observed, "The Irish and the Ukrainians in this town have always disliked one another. Now they're calling one another names again! I can't believe it!"[44]

The Borough Council moved quickly to deny the CC access to the Borough Hall for its meetings. Council members agreed, with one dissenting vote, to close its doors to the CC as a disruptive influence on the town. In a public meeting, the president of council said: "I'm appalled the people in the Catholic Church who approve such grants would give this money to Concerned Citizens. . . . The name of your organization is appropriate. All residents of this town have a right to be concerned about your organization."[45]

CC members had no idea that the grant would create such conflict in town. Indeed, how could they? The group did not have a clear idea what the grant was for. After the money was awarded, personnel from both the Campaign for Human Development and CSS came to a CC meeting to describe the purpose of the award. Recognizing the volatile atmosphere that the grant had created, CSS suggested to the CC that it invite members of the Borough Council to attend the meeting. An excerpt from the minutes of the CC meeting reflects the tension: "[CSS] attempted to explain the Grant and showed a film titled 'With One Voice.' . . . Father K. attempted to explain the grant . . . but not to the satisfaction of certain ones in attendance."[46] Indeed, the exchanges between certain members of council and representatives of the funding agency became so emotional that several people walked out of the meeting.

The work done by organizers for the Rural American Women and by CSS in securing a grant that the CC did not even understand suggests that it is very difficult for these organizations to modify their normative approach to community organizing to meet the unique challenge posed by a chronic technological disaster.[47]

On November 9, less than a month after the grant was awarded, the CC officers, with the exception of the president, resigned amidst bitter controversy. Interim officers were appointed, but for all practical purposes the CC became a paper organization. Quarterly meetings were scheduled, but only a handful of people attended. The fact that the group did not

officially disband, however, would pose serious problems for the
second major grassroots group to emerge, the Centralia Committee on Human Development.

A former CC officer reflected on why she and the others
resigned: "I was tired. We all were. All that seemed to be happening was one squabble after another. I still think the grant
was a good idea. We were all just tired of the struggle." As the
following exchange makes clear, "the struggle" that was exhaust-
ing the group and others in town was not against the fire but
with neighbors and former friends who, over the course of several
months, had become bitter enemies. A telling exchange between
a former resident of Centralia, active in the CC, who was forced
to relocate because of the fire, and a member of Borough Council:

CC: You told me to keep my kids out of town, my wife out of town,
    and me out of town. . . . I don't want that to happen again.
Councilman: I never said that.
CC: Yes you did. You called me and told me to keep my kids and
    wife out of town.
Councilman: You're full of it.[48]

For most Centralians, the disaster was now above ground, not
below.

6. A Thwarted Struggle for Unity

For one and a half years, the Concerned Citizens struggled to persuade the political system and their own neighbors that the mine fire represented a serious threat to health and safety and to the well-being of the community. The activist group helped to bring Centralia to the attention of the state and federal governments, and generated the kind of public sympathy conducive to political action. Moreover, the CC's trips to Washington and Harrisburg were effective tactics in pushing the mine fire toward the front of political concern. Their constant reminders that the government's responsibility to protect health and safety went beyond mere observation and measurement of a mine fire kept moral pressure on legislators and agency directors to be accountable to the needs of Centralians. It is reasonable to assume that relief from technological hazards of chronic duration depends in part upon the persistent reiteration of worst-case scenarios to keep public interest alive.

The success of the CC with political powers remote from the borough must be measured against its marked failure to organize the town around its beliefs. The only allies it won in its brief existence were reporters and social service agencies—sectors outside the local structure that had vested interests in adopting a worst-case interpretation.

Centralians who lived outside the direct path of the fire found it much easier to deny the CC's warnings of the threat—particularly since the admission of that threat would have jeopardized the very existence of their community. What could not be ignored were the severe emotional disturbances that disrupted collective life. For most Centralians, the rancorous conflict that developed between the hot and cold sides of town became more anxiety-provoking than the fire itself. "It's my neighbor," observed one man, "and not the fire, that bothers me most."

Against this backdrop of mounting hostility, the government-sponsored borehole study began to reveal some startling figures. As if fed by the social hatred above ground, the fire began to spread rapidly. In September of 1982, twenty years after the fire was discovered, Pennsylvania Department of Environmental Resources personnel were still refusing to speculate publicly whether or not the fire was in fact within the boundaries of the borough. On October 1, however, officials admitted in a public meeting that the DER and the OSM had been aware since May that the fire had advanced within the boundaries of the borough. It is not clear why the government did not tell Centralians earlier; what is clear is that the imperfect hazard management strategies of government had cut the community off from the opportunity to respond effectively to the peril.

On October 5, basing its story on borehole temperature readings being collected by the government, the local newspaper reported, "New borehole results show that the . . . mine fire is advancing into the borough along a 200-foot front." "A 'gigantic fire,' " the paper reported the following day, "part of the . . . Centralia mine fire—is fast approaching the village of Byrnesville south of Centralia."[1] On October 14, the Pennsylvania Emergency Management Agency announced that tests of several homes on the south end of Centralia, east and west of Locust Avenue, had determined them to be endangered by fire-related gases.

"It's hell on earth," exclaimed one young mother. Another woman, whose 20-inch-thick basement walls had recently cracked in the heat from the fire, lamented, "I can't sleep. I'm coughing all night. You just wonder if you're going to be the one sacrificed." An engineer employed by the OSM sympathized with the residents on the south end of town: "[They] have been on borrowed time for a long time. It's only been a miracle that there hasn't been a loss of life. . . . Something has to be done. Do you have to wait for five people to die in bed?"[2]

As the fire heated up below ground, tempers flamed above. For many in town, the affront of the CC's grant from the Campaign for Human Development eclipsed even the bad news that the fire was spreading. The resignations of the CC officers in November of 1982 surprised Catholic Social Services and sent it scurrying to fill the vacant offices. Survival of the CC itself was not at issue for CSS; the primary concern was the survival of the grant. The agency, and the Harrisburg diocese it represented, would suffer not a little embarrassment if a grant had to be withdrawn only weeks after it was awarded, because the recipient group had collapsed under the community's antagonism toward the grant. From the ranks of the CC's membership, a slate of temporary officers was drawn up. This new group, including a young Russian Orthodox priest known regionally for his skills at conflict resolution, would take over the grant. Having completed its backstage management of the death of the CC and the birth of a successor to administer the grant, CSS was content to step back and watch its investment.

The fledgling five-member group, charged with managing what for many was a considerable sum of money, began its career with a serious handicap: since the $30,000 grant had been awarded to the organization named Concerned Citizens, the new group's official name must include the words "concerned citizens." (This label would hamper many of the new group's efforts to reorganize the coping style of the community.) It was clear that the new group needed a new name before it could attempt to forge an identity independent of the CC, as the minutes from its first meeting attest: "Discussion ensued on the advisability of Concerned Citizens being part of the title, and it was pointed out that the grant was awarded to Concerned Citizens and the name of the organization must be included, although it could be played down and put in smaller print." The Russian Orthodox priest, seeking to influence the meaning and purpose of the group, suggested calling it the Centralia Committee on Human Development. It was decided that the organization's letterhead would read:

CENTRALIA COMMITTEE ON HUMAN DEVELOPMENT
A project of concerned citizens

The humanistic, nonpartisan ring of this name promised a new approach to the mine fire crises.

Meeting on a weekly basis, the CCHD began to take shape, although not without considerable bickering and maneuvering for advantage. In fact, the first few CCHD meetings bordered on chaos. Accustomed to CC-style meetings given over to expressions of fear and anger, CCHD members spoke at random, interrupting one another, lobbying for their particular solutions to the problem. The first several assemblies began at 7:00 in the evening and finally broke up four or five hours later, having accomplished nothing substantial. The group knew that the mandate of the grant was to build a coalition of residents to make government accountable for the health and safety of Centralians. But, as the following excerpt from the minutes of an early meeting make clear, some members of the CCHD had other ideas about their goal: "Some committee members felt that to halt all direct action until the community is organized would be self-defeating, and the community is more likely to join a successful group, rather than yet another group that is floundering."[4]

In other words, some members were more inclined to push for a solution to the fire than to organize a town. After all, hadn't their predecessors tried to build a community organization, only to be contemptuously rebuked time and again? In an apparent effort to align themselves with CCHD members who advocated seeking a more direct solution to the fire than organizing the town, several former CC officers asked the CCHD to use the money to sue Borough Council and other levels of government. One CCHD member, in apparent exasperation, explained that she would rather "spend her personal time and energy in combating these problems . . . rather than attempting to organize a community which other groups have already attempted to without success."[5] The fire was not waiting for CCHD to become organized, nor for Centralia to become organized.

The minutes of one CCHD meeting sum up the gloomy feeling

members shared as they faced the task of building an organization: "No optimism was demonstrated, no strategies offered, no
methods were suggested."⁶ The suggestion to use the grant
money to hire an attorney became a critical issue in the first
several weeks of the group's existence; fighting various levels of
government in court would be a logical extension of the CC's
struggle with recalcitrant authorities who would not accept its
worst-case interpretation of the fire. The question of whether or
not to use grant money to pursue litigation became a contest of
wills between the two members who viewed confrontation as the
most promising route to crises resolution and those who wanted
instead to forge a model for communal action.

At one CCHD meeting, a motion was formally made to "hire,
as soon as possible, an attorney . . . in order to balance CCHD
with Borough Council."⁷ The motion was resisted, in open hostility among several group members. After several meetings,
CCHD members realized that their group was nothing more
than a mirror image of the town: fractured, easily goaded into
confrontation, incapable of working collectively. The volatile,
antagonistic interpersonal exchanges that characterized the first
several meetings of the group were of serious concern to the
priest who had agreed to sit on the committee. He challenged
the group to put aside its differences, threatening to quit if the
direction of the committee did not change appreciably. Out of
deference to his vocation, members appointed him chairman of
the group, a move CSS had hoped would occur.

It was apparent to everyone, not just the clergyman, that the
group must first change its pattern of interaction, its group dynamic. If Centralians as a whole were going to put aside their
differences and work together, they needed at the very least a
model for communal action. The CC and Borough Council had
served only as models of self-destruction. A principal goal of the
new group would be to serve Centralia as a credible model of
communal organization, available within the town. But first the
group would have to learn to resolve its own disputes peacefully.

At the request of the chairman, members agreed to conduct themselves during a CCHD meeting according to three basic rules that would later prove effective in organizing the town into neighborhood meetings. The rules were: only one person could speak at a time; other members were forbidden to interrupt the person speaking; and members were prohibited from criticizing one another for the ideas they presented.

Each CCHD member agreed to abide by these rules, and gradually meetings became more orderly affairs, where whoever was speaking was respectfully attended to and differences were expressed and resolved (or left as differences) in a context of mutual respect. When it became clear to the two committee members given to a confrontational approach that not only were they unable to convert the group to their preferred strategy, but that the volatile emotions of anger and fear were not going to be entertained during CCHD meetings, they resigned. They were replaced by two hot-side residents who had also been active CC members.

Partly in reaction to the two former members' inclination toward confrontation, the CCHD realized that it must reach a common understanding of itself as a group, by which all members would abide. Recognizing that it had no allies in its attempts to suppress hostile outbursts and mobilize residents, the CCHD decided to forgo any public activity until the group itself had worked out a method of conflict resolution. If the CCHD was to become a model for reorganization of the town, it must first tend to its own internal workings. Although the group had formed in November of 1982, it was not until the end of March 1983 that it first sponsored a public meeting.[8]

When the CCHD discussed the volatile exchanges that had marked its first several meetings, the young cleric warned that continued expressions of rank discord would demoralize the group. He asked members not to deny the reality of the mine fire and the threats it posed (real or otherwise), but to isolate whatever emotions the fire triggered, at least while participating in the group. He asked that members discourage one another from emotional displays and excited discussions of the dangers of the fire.

In a logical extension of its decision not to discuss the fire in the language of fear, the group agreed to refrain from adopting a definition of the fire as either a threat or a nuisance, and from attempting to convert the town to its interpretation. Unlike its predecessor and the other groups that would emerge in the next year, the CCHD adopted a policy of noninterpretation. Unable to address the source of the threat and unwilling to respond emotionally to it, this fledgling group took the high ground of nonpartisanship. Members agreed not to address the mine fire, its potential effect on health and safety, or the method of dealing with it, in terms of any of the reductionist definitions extant within the town. One member summed up the reasoning of the group: "We are not engineers. There's a mine fire problem, but we aren't DER . . . so why should we be running around trying to tell everybody where the fire is and how bad the gases are?" As we shall see, this strategy of noninterpretation, aimed at controlling the volatile emotions of group members and other Centralians, would prove an elusive goal, more suitable for individual tension management than community problem-solving.

Rather than set forth a specific interpretation of the fire and adopt a confrontational coping style, the CCHD decided to position itself within the community to help the conflicting parties address their emotional responses to the threat and reach a mutually satisfactory settlement of differences, as stated in the group's quarterly report to the funding agency: "We have no technical experience to determine what option would best address the mine fire. . . . Since we are not qualified to address the technical problems in dealing with the fire, we centered our efforts around keeping the borough as much intact as possible."[9]

The CCHD sought to use the political leverage that comes from nonalignment to become a mediator in the town. Taking the perspective of the community as a social unit, rather than focusing on any single section's interpretation of the fire, it was clear that neighborhoods were experiencing very different levels of stress and social disruption. Adopting the motto "We're all hurting but in different ways," the group sought to convince the conflicting parties that no one living in Centralia was escaping the pain and turmoil. The essential task the CCHD set for itself was to direct the attention of the community away from the fire and toward what it perceived as a disaster of even greater magnitude: the social destruction of the borough.

Within a few weeks of its first meeting, the emergent group had hammered out an ambitious agenda, including a mandate to adopt none of the interpretations of the fire, to become a model for communal affiliation and thus position itself as a mediator group, and to influence the terms that Centralians used to discuss and define the crises.[10]

Although it was not until March that the CCHD held its first public meeting, the group was very active during the preceding months. Its strategy—to redefine the terms of the conflict while serving as a model for conflict resolution—encouraged the CCHD to look for ways to address what it perceived to be the real crises in town. After a vigorous discussion of possible courses of action, the minutes of one meeting concluded by noting: "Committee agreed [that the] course of action now is how to help the *people*, not the fire."[11]

The CCHD decided first to investigate the possibility of establishing a mental health unit in town. A call to the county mental health services agency revealed that thirteen Centralians had sought assistance in managing emotional problems in the past eight months, or double the number who routinely sought such help. The CCHD members suggested that, since the forty-five-minute drive from Centralia to the mental health office probably deterred many other residents, a mental health resource in Centralia itself would encourage residents to examine the costs of the social hatred they lived with day to day. The CCHD persuaded the county agency to apply to the state Department of Public Welfare for a grant to establish a mental health satellite in Centralia, which opened its doors in May of 1983, staffed by a secretary and a therapist. At first, residents were reluctant to be seen walking into the facility for fear of neighbors' gossip. But gradually more and more Centralians sought the services of the clinic, which acquired a reputation in town as an anxiety-reducing resource. People also began to talk favorably about the CCHD, the group that had provided the town with a noncontroversial, problem-solving resource.

The CCHD acquired a wider reputation when its chairman and others spoke via the local radio station about the human problems facing the town, during a weekly program that originated in a community four miles from Centralia. Using a call-in format, giving Centralians an opportunity to comment or ask questions, the show focused on the human costs of the crisis. Included among the topics were the roles of rumor and gossip, the health and psychological costs of chronic conflict among neighbors, and the multiple ways in which everyone in town was affected by the fire.

Recognizing that Centralia's youth were victims of the community conflict, the CCHD paid for refurbishing the town's Teen Center and making it a more attractive place for teenagers to congregate. To reach those of all ages, the CCHD in February 1983 hired as coordinator a Roman Catholic nun who was experienced in organizing southern Appalachian groups. The sister began by visiting Centralians in their homes and simply listening, as she put it, "to anything that was on their minds." Her purpose was "not to persuade but to support."

It was becoming clear to Centralians that the CCHD was approaching the crisis in a fashion quite different from that of the CC or the Borough Council. The mental health clinic and the radio program encouraged residents to rearrange their interpretation of the problems besetting Centralia. The remodeling of the Teen Center and the coordinator's door-to-door visits reminded Centralians that youth and neighbor were important to them as a community. The chairman of the CCHD was well aware that not only was the group meeting basic needs in town, but it was also acquiring a reputation for nonpartisanship that would help it play the role of mediator. As the group worked to position itself as an organization independent of the prevailing factions in town, it was also developing internally as a consensus group, a model for communal association.

The resources the CCHD introduced into Centralia were appreciated by many, but they did not result in attachment to the group. The mine fire had become a volatile emotional issue that did not lend itself to reflection and reconsideration. In a typical response, a former councilman said, "I appreciate what this group is doing for the town, but the real issue is the fire and nobody around here thinks otherwise." Another man, referring to the money the CCHD had donated to the Teen Center, commented: "They have a lot of money to spend. It doesn't surprise me that they're giving it away." Expressing the incapacity of most residents to trust in the benevolent intentions of their neighbors, another man condemned the group's unselfish behavior as nothing more than a front to hide its real intentions: selling the town to coal companies for a profit.

It was difficult for most Centralians to accept that a group would seek to be noncontroversial, concerned only about the welfare of the community. Because it would not come down on one side or the other of the conflicting interpretations, the CCHD was a difficult group with which to identify: its greatest asset, its nonpartisan position, was also its greatest deficit. Borough Council members, former members of the CC, and many other felt a need to attribute blame for the social demoralization of their town; attributions help to explain events. Beyond that, blame attribution, as we shall see, sets the accused off from the rest, investing the accusers with a semblance of control over their predicament.[12] The CCHD seemed to be saying to everyone, "Live with the ambiguity of the mine fire and let's address together the bitterness of your neighbor." This would prove difficult for most residents, who were without the support of an intimate group like the CCHD to nurture patience and benevolence. In the end, in a desperate effort to bring residents together, the CCHD would respond to the community's predilection for emotional displays, embroiling itself in the town's vicious cycle of blame attribution.

The internal structure of the CCHD was not the only factor that inhibited its acceptance by most Centralians. As the continuing advance of the fire increased the antagonism in town, competing groups emerged, each expressing its own vested interest in the outcome of the crisis.

Within two months of the founding of the CCHD, a small group numbering no more than ten active members formed in the adjacent village of Byrnesville, a community of twenty-five families one-half mile south of Centralia. By all accounts, Byrnesville was in the direct path of the advance of the fire. Calling themselves the Citizens to Save Byrnesville, this group began to meet secretly, permitting no outside access to their deliberations, even by the press. The group made little effort to establish a liaison between itself and groups in Centralia. A founding member's explanations for this strategy of isolation is instructive: "When the DER said the fire was coming our way, we knew we had a big problem. We felt the press wouldn't help us. Our local paper confuses people and distorts things. We didn't seek any help from Centralia because they can't even help themselves. Look at Council, they can't agree on when to hold a workshop. And no one wants anything to do with the CC, or that new group [the CCHD]."

The Citizens to Save Byrnesville adamantly rejected the fire as being a serious threat to anybody. Several families in Byrnesville refused to have their homes monitored for gases, against the recommendation of the Pennsylvania Department of Health. Indeed, in the face of mounting evidence that the fire was moving south toward their village, residents scoffed at the idea that they were endangered. In the words of a member of the Save Byrnesville group, the real threat to Byrnesville was not the fire but "a bunch of assholes in Centralia that think they're going to get some money from the government at my expense. I'll die here before I see that happen."

Convinced that their neighbors "up the hill" were to blame

for the troubles they were experiencing, the Citizens to Save Byrnesville disrupted several public meetings in Centralia, shouting down anyone who expressed an opinion differing from their own. Indeed, as one member revealed, this "shout down" strategy was formally adopted by the group to ensure that its interpretation of the problem received public attention. It is also possible that these hostile outbursts were related to the coping style of the group: it makes little sense to scream at an underground fire, but when the "real" sources of misery are human agents violating moral standards, venting hostile impulses appears quite reasonable. Externalizing blame by attributing reprehensible characteristics to others, the residents of Byrnesville had no trouble in explaining why their lives were so seriously disrupted.

Although the Citizens to Save Byrnesville exacerbated the tensions in Centralia, the group played a relatively minor role in the complexity of events during the mine fire crisis. The group did, however, serve as a model for—in fact, merged with—a Centralia group that organized in the latter weeks of August 1983: Citizens to Save the Borough. Moreover, although the CC and the Citizens to Save could not have been further apart in opinions on the scope and severity of the fire, both groups practiced confrontation and blame attribution. This convergence of coping styles between two groups that held diametrically opposed views of the fire illustrates our central idea that it was the way people responded to one another's attempts to make sense out of the underground fire that constituted the real disaster in Centralia.

As federal and state governments continued their borehole study to determine the perimeter of the fire and devise a plan to stop it, heat from the mine fire was disrupting the daily lives of many people. In early January 1983, underground heat cracked the state highway running north and south through the borough. The crack across the highway, roughly 10 feet long, occurred in the impact zone at the southern edge of town. Mining maps of the area under the crack showed that mining had robbed the pillars of coal, removing the support of the highway. A natural gas pipeline adjacent to the highway became a serious concern when temperature readings under the highway climbed above 770°F. Few people were reassured by the government's pronouncement that the natural gas pipeline had been built to withstand temperatures in excess of 1,000°F. On a cloudy or damp day, steam from the fire rose on either side of the highway, engulfing the road and reducing visibility to zero. A DER official summed up: "We have a pretty nasty situation along Route 61. There is not a lot of cover, there's a big void and high temperatures."[13]

In the course of several days, 9,000 tons of fly ash barrier were pumped into the ground under the highway at a cost exceeding $330,000. But the heat under the road did not abate. The 10-foot crack widened, and steam continued to belch from the ground, hovering over the road like a dense fog. After a rear-end collision involving a DER state vehicle, the state closed the highway, one of the region's major thoroughfares. Sawhorses placed end to end with flashing yellow lights strapped to their crossbars confronted those travelers who ignored the 200 or more detour signs in the area and drove to the site of the subsidence. A twenty-four-hour police watch kept an eye on the barricade.

As the government was closing the highway, interrupting the travel of thousands of area residents, two families on the hill awoke one morning to a thunderous, reverberating crash that shook the houses when a cave-in tore out pieces of their basement walls. A few weeks before, a subsidence had occurred in the basement of an adjacent house. Subsidences had torn up yards and fields before, but these were the first recorded incidents of fissures under homes.

Frightening as the latest cave-ins must have been for families on the hill, it is doubtful that many cold-side community residents would have reacted forcefully to these incidents alone. The closing of Route 61, however, was a major inconvenience to many Centralians who now had to drive more than six miles to reach a neighboring town that before had been only one mile away.

The rerouting of school buses forced families to rearrange their morning and evening schedules. Routine was disrupted every Sunday for the Roman Catholic majority in town, who attended mass at Saint Ignatius church on the southern edge of the borough, no more than thirty yards from the roadblock. It was one thing for a few families to complain about gases and subsidences in their homes; it was quite another for everyone in town to be inconvenienced and made anxious by the closing of a major thoroughfare. Within days after the highway was closed, a new group emerged in town, calling for unity.

The timing was right. The community still lacked a viable organization through which residents could put concerted pressure on state and federal governments. The CC was now little more than a memory, although a vivid one. The CCHD was still developing internally, and the Citizens to Save Byrnesville could hardly serve as a foundation for collective action in Centralia. The Borough Council itself was mired in internal squabbles, not to mention the day-to-day business of running the borough.

At a community meeting set up by Pennsylvania agencies responsible for closing Route 61, several Centralians expressed the desire to start a new community group to attack the seemingly endless problems associated with the fire. In yet another attempt to band together, some forty citizens representing all areas of Centralia, as well as Byrnesville, gathered on January 20, 1983, at Borough Hall. The United Centralia Area Mine Fire Task Force, as they decided to call themselves, was to focus both on the community conflict and on federal and state funding—after the results of the borehole study were made public.

The discord and animosity in town was of concern to everyone at the first meeting of the Task Force. The question of how to overcome the divisiveness, reduce the misunderstanding, and establish a common cause was the first task at hand. A retired priest in the group recommended that a day be set aside for the expression of unity—a day dedicated to reaffirming Centralians' commitment to one another and their town. The whirlwind of activity that followed promised at first to heal the divisions in town. Neighbor worked with neighbor on the various concrete tasks necessary to, as one man put it, "strike up the band and announce to everyone that the town is united."

In the weeks that followed, Task Force members asked voluntary associations in town, including the Fire Company Auxiliary, the Teen Club, and the American Legion, to help in planning the day. Neighboring communities were invited. A Task Force petition was circulated not only within the region but throughout the nation, where more than 10,000 names were signed beneath these words:

SET CENTRALIA FREE IN '83

I/We the undersigned, urgently request the allocation of funding necessary to expedite work on the mine fire immediately following the completion of the . . . borehole drilling project.

Several committees, set up to manage the practical side of sponsoring a day of unity, worked in apparent harmony to arrange refreshment, transportation, press releases, and fund raising. The process of planning Unity Day was a noncontroversial, anxiety-reducing experience that served to inhibit the display of conflict. Even in such a unifying activity, however, differences between residents were not entirely suppressed, as the following fieldnote indicates: "Immediately after————announces that St. Ignatius church would be the setting for one part of Unity Day events, a woman interrupted the speaker to say that many people will refuse to go into St. Ignatius because it is an Irish church." After a lengthy debate on whether or not any church in town would be acceptable to all Centralians, St. Ignatius was chosen because it was Centralia's largest church and close to the barricades blocking Route 61.

A few differences over the nitty-gritty details of staging the Unity Day event, however, did not fragment the group; cooperation in this expression of unity was paramount. Indeed, an elderly woman found the whole affair "most different for us. I see people working together who last week wouldn't speak [to one another]." People compared the planning of Unity Day to the planning of Centralia's centennial celebration in 1969. Many residents recalled the staging of the town's one-hundredth birthday celebration as the most recent social event that involved the whole town, rather than just a single auxiliary or parish.

During the weeks leading up to Unity Day, many Centralians were optimistic that their town was healing itself as it prepared for an occasion arguably more significant than its centennial party. Even during the early stages, however, there were portents of troubles to come, notably the spatial arrangement at the United Committee Task Force meetings, which mirrored a community history bereft of a tradition of concerted action in a crisis.

At each meeting of the Task Force, there were at least twenty people who had committed themselves to some task associated with staging the event. Those who were immediately involved in planning activities sat at the front of the room around the outside of long rectangular tables arranged in a square open on one end. The thirty-five-foot distance between Task Force members on opposite sides of the square created problems in simple communication. People were frequently asked to repeat themselves because others could not hear them. The distance between members also encouraged those sitting near one another to withdraw from group discussions and engage in two- or three-person conversations, oblivious to what was occurring around them. It was not uncommon for two, three, even four separate conversations to be in progress while the leader of the group was attempting to direct attention to the issue under discussion.

A strong leader might have been able to link the separate groups in communication, but the Task Force had decided against formal leadership, in the name of cooperation and, as one man put it, "to be a democratic organization." Someone, however, had to moderate, open and close the meetings, bring issues to the floor for discussion, and move the group along in its meeting agenda. The role of moderator shifted between members of council and the mayor. Eschewing a leadership role, the moderators had difficulty in claiming the group's attention, and they frequently admonished members for not cooperating by discussing the concerns that had been introduced. Not only did the moderators fail to assert leadership, but the group itself would not allow the moderator's role to shift to one of leadership. At one point in a particularly uncoordinated meeting, the mayor, acting as moderator, attempted to claim the position of his elected office to redirect the group. "I'm your mayor," he began, "I must have your attention. We have business to conduct." One member of the group was quick to respond, "You're not mayor of this meeting!"

This loosely structured organization nevertheless managed to function adequately as it concentrated on Unity Day. Planning transportation for the elderly, circulating the petition, organizing a hoagie sale to raise money, planning the agenda for the day, and notifying the press of the schedule—the group accomplished all this within a matter of five weeks. During this planning period, there was practically no discussion of the fire, its scope, or its seriousness.

March 7, 1983, was Unity Day. Accounts vary, but it is estimated that five hundred people, Centralians and others from neighboring communities, participated in the event.[14] The day began with a nondenominational ceremony at the Roman Catholic church, followed by a march from the church to Borough Hall initiated by the release of several hundred helium-filled balloons, and over two hours of speeches and activities and the hall. Several politicians and regional dignitaries addressed the need for a united Centralia:[15]

In the unity that is shown here by the men and the women and the children of Centralia coming together, you have made a beginning in doing what must be done.—Congressman Frank Harrison

I would urge you not to make this just Unity Day, but the first day of a great unity movement.—R. ("Bud") Dwyer, former Pennsylvania State treasurer

I know you're hearing a lot of good words from a lot of speakers, but when it comes down to it, it is going to be you yourselves who are going to be able to effectuate a change in the . . . mine fire.— Richard Kulick, international auditor, United Mine Workers of America

Be candid with each other. Be fair with each other. Be sensitive with each other and employ common sense in the solution of problems for which no perfect solutions exist.—General DeWitt Smith, director of the Pennsylvania Emergency Management Agency

These words made sense to residents on both sides of town. The wise counsel offered by representatives of powerful organizations concerned about the plight of the town coincided with the perceived need of many Centralians for a broad-based coalition to demand relief from the social and ecological ravages of the fire. To recognize a need, however, is only the first step in creating a communal organization. The next critical step is developing an organizational means of persuading people that action governed by criteria of mutual respect and common belonging is preferable to rank discord.

Unity Day was a successful media event in terms of the dramatic, though temporary, expression of unanimity. But in the end, it could not serve as the foundation for collective action to rescue the town from the underground fire. Without such a model, the Unity Committee was left with only the blueprint for group action that had typified the town's twenty-one-year response to the fire. The results were disastrous.

On March 8, the day after Unity Day, the Unity Committee held a meeting, chaired by the Borough Council president. The seating arrangement was again a square open at the end facing the audience. Unlike the pattern of previous meetings, however, when members distributed themselves around the tables in an ad hoc fashion, the post–unity day seating expressed the social cleavages within the borough. As if anticipating the need for group support, Unity Committee members sat next to those whose interpretations of the scope and seriousness of the fire were similar to their own. The three members of the committee who had remained neutral on the issue of the correct interpretation of the crisis huddled together at the end of one table. As the meeting progressed, the spatial distance between residents symbolized, in spite of the apparent strides made on Unity Day, their continuing personal and social differences.

For the first forty-five minutes of the meeting, the committee congratulated itself on having planned and staged Unity Day. Then, taking advantage of a lull in discussion, the chairman brought this segment of the meeting to an abrupt end with the comment, "Okay, now that all the backslapping is done, let's get down to business." Sensing that he now had the group's full attention, he asked, "Should we be chartered?"

A cacophonous debate ensued. Someone suggested that a charter was needed if the group was to seek federal grant money. Someone else shot back, "Why do we need federal grant money? I'm against looking for grants." The discord lasted for several minutes, until one man succeeded in introducing another issue, leaving the question of the charter unresolved; the Unity Committee remained unchartered by default. The group switched to the question of whether or not the Unity Committee should work closely with the OSM and the DER to impress upon them the needs of the community. The vice president of the Borough Council responded quickly that this was the proper task of the local government, not the Unity Committee.

The discussion then drifted to a proposal by one woman that Centralians charter busses and travel to Washington to meet with Interior Secretary Watt. Sharp objections were expressed to the propriety of this suggestion. When one man revealed that he had written Secretary Watt requesting a meeting, the mayor angrily denounced him for acting without the consent of the group. The man explained that he had been asked by one of the Unity Day subcommittees to write the letter. Angry words were exchanged, and the meeting had all but collapsed when several elderly women who had been sitting in the audience rose and announced that they were going to leave if this hostile exchange continued.

Tempers subsided for a brief time. The borough solicitor then accused several former CC members of trying to acquire properties in the impact zone to sell at inflated prices should a government buy-out occur. A young woman stood up and tried to explain that the CC was in the process of reorganization, that although the old group had disbanded, the conditions of the social service grant required the CC to remain in existence, if only on paper. Ignoring her explanation of the status of the CC, the attorney announced loudly, "I do not want you to make decisions that will affect me against my will." Angry and embarrassed at her treatment by the solicitor, the young woman walked out of the meeting. A few minutes later, the mayor asked a priest in attendance to give the closing prayer.

Had the Unity Committee attempted simply to manage the melange of conflicting emotions about the "real" threat of the fire by holding further expressive events to dramatize unity, it might have minimized internal conflict. That might have been a more reasonable strategy for the committee. In any case, the group's shift from emotion management to problem solving brought the Unity Committee up against the insoluble. Communal affiliation was devalued in favor of one or another interpretation of the crisis, a form of radical subjectivity that would express itself throughout the career of the group.

At the next meeting, a resident of the impact zone, who adamantly rejected any suggestion that the fire was dangerous, suggested in good faith that families with gas monitors remove the devices from their homes and deposit them at the steps of the local DER office. Such an act, she argued, would attract media attention and force the government to respond. A young man whose children were experiencing chronic upper respiratory problems diagnosed by a physician as CO_2-related, found the suggestion ludicrous. As a parent, he argued, he would be irresponsible to remove the gas monitor from his home. The woman who had made the suggestion countered: "I, for one, have no gases in my home. And I have a strong feeling that if we turn in the monitors, we will force them to do something." The young father responded, "How on earth do you know whether or not you have gases if you don't have a monitor?"

A week later the group met again, this time to read aloud and discuss a letter that had been drafted to Secretary Watt. One woman suggested deleting the sentence "We want the fire put out under any conditions." She argued that this phrase would signal to the government that the group favored any means to extinguish the fire, even if that meant destroying the town. A caustic exchange followed in which some residents accused others of caring more about the town than about human health and safety. Their opponents claimed that the fire could be managed without destroying the town and that those who thought otherwise were not interested in the welfare of the community. "I'm not selling my house to save any of you," one man shouted. Another man yelled back, "Save yourself. I'll take care of my business!" At one point in this volatile discussion, the suggestion was made to put the issue to a vote. One of those who objected to a vote argued that it would be "undemocratic."

In exchanges such as these, residents became aware that whatever common ground there might have been at one time had all but disappeared as factions desperately defended their own individual interpretations of the crisis. Strategies and proposals were evaluated not on the basis of intrinsic merits, but simply on the grounds of who had suggested them. Uncompromising adherence to any exclusionary interpretation of the fire precluded behavior governed by criteria of common belonging.

In a perhaps foreseeable turn of events, committee meetings began to attract fewer and fewer residents from the south end of town. "We've got enough grief with council and DER," reasoned one resident of the impact zone, "I don't need to go to these crazy Unity meetings anymore." With the steady attrition of residents from the south end of town, the Unity Committee came to represent, not multiple interpretations, but the single firm belief that the fire was a problem, not a crisis. It resembled both the CC and the Citizens to Save Byrnesville in being organized around a unilateral understanding of the fire, ready to call anyone who disagreed with its interpretation not only a deficient witness to reality, but morally suspect.

The Unity Committee continued to meet biweekly through July 1983, primarily to plan a community trip to Washington, even though letters sent to Interior Secretary Watt requesting a meeting went unanswered. Although there was general agreement on the worth of a trip to the capital, the group could not agree on what it would do once it got there. The suggestion of inviting a former CC member to advise on what they might do in Washington was roundly condemned. In a bitter tone, one woman flatly stated that she would "have nothing to do with that group." "Whatever we do," observed one member, "we have to look like professionals when we go to Washington. Or they're going to think we're a bunch of hicks." It was his proposal that the committee "buy an easel and draw up a lot of charts that could be flipped back and forth during our presentation." These props, he argued, would help the group convince "the bureaucrats in Washington that we mean business." Several members of the group responded enthusiastically but others were more realistic. One asked, with more than a touch of wryness, "And what do we put on these charts that we flip around?" A more basic question followed: "What do we want?" It was this fundamental question that the Unity Committee failed to collectively answer.

Nor did the Unity Committee ever make it to Washington. Secretary Watt's refusal to answer the inquiries puzzled the group. Recalling a brother who had received a letter from President Gerald Ford in response to an inquiry about physical fitness, one man could not understand why a "secretary" would refuse to answer their letters. On this score, at least, veterans of the CC could have helped the committee. The obvious lack of communication between members of the two groups meant, in effect, that the Unity Committee was destined to repeat the failures of the CC. It finally became apparent that Watt had no intention of corresponding with the Unity Committee.

In one of the last meetings of the group, resignation, frustration, and feelings of impotence were openly expressed. "Maybe we should not hope to see Watt," commented one woman. Another agreed: "Maybe if we see a deputy secretary or an undersecretary, that will do." "What makes you think we're going to see anybody in Washington?" asked the mayor. Throwing his hands in the air, another man asked angrily, "And if we get to Washington and if we see even the President, what are we going to say? We don't even know what we're going to say." "We're a democratic group," counseled another member. "We should say what the community wants us to say." "What is that?" two or three people asked almost in unison. "We want the fire out. That's what we want," affirmed an elderly man. "We're not a decision-making group," countered another member. "If we start making decisions for everybody, I'm walking out now. I'll be no part of a group that thinks it can make decisions for the community." In a loud and exasperated voice, one man quelled the discussion as if he had caught the group doing something shameful: "I'm always hearing now when I go out of town, 'What's wrong with the people in Centralia? Why can't they do something about their problem?' I tell you, if they were here now they would soon find out."

The failure of the Unity Committee can be traced to several factors, including its acephalous structure (leadership being passed around from meeting to meeting); its tendency to fracture along preexisting differences regarding the "real" sources of threat and conflict in the borough; and a painfully obvious lack of agreed-upon rules for appropriate conduct at the meetings. The Unity Committee was mistaken in assuming that a single day set aside for unity would heal the deep-seated divisions in town. Having achieved Unity Day, members felt that they could resolve their crisis by appealing to a common identity and shared rules for corporate problem solving. When the Unity Committee shifted from staging an event to the politics of the mine fire, the group divided into competing factions, each blaming the other for the common problems of the uncommon fire.

The failure of the Unity Committee to accomplish anything beyond Unity Day was a clear signal to many that even the unanimity of reaction to the closing of a vital highway was not enough to unite Centralians. "Nothing works in this town," mused one man, "not even us."

7. One Town, Many Groups

In late March 1983, as the Unity Committee was facing the true difficulties of forging a cooperative organization, and as the Centralia Committee For Human Development was planning its first public meeting, the federal Office of Surface Mining released an interim report from the borehole study, which was then in the final stages. Based on examination of 189 boreholes, the report noted: "The high temperature area (400-1000°F) covers a larger area than was originally conceived." Of the sixty-seven borehole temperature readings listed in the report, forty-one were higher than normal, some hitting 1000°F.[1]

The borehole study not only revealed a dilemma much worse than originally thought, but by itself threatened the health of some residents, since a few of the boreholes were venting CO and CO_2 into nearby houses. In one home a few hundred feet from a borehole, the gas monitor registered a CO level of 14 parts per million for twelve consecutive hours; the official thresholds for dangerous exposure were 9 ppm for nine hours or 35 ppm for one hour. Other families, too, complained of elevated gas readings after boreholes were drilled near their properties.

In early April, the fire broke cover in a ravine, visible to sightseers who were curious enough to climb a sharp incline and then peer downward. Supported by sensory evidence and official intelligence, the fire became more and more difficult to deny. Within a period of three weeks, four subsidences were discovered in Centralia and one occurred a few hundred yards away, in Byrnesville. The Byrnesville subsidence, 20 by 15 feet across and 30 feet deep, severed the water line into the village, depriving Byrnesville of running water for several days. Only a few days later, two more holes in the earth opened up in Centralia. Even the county emergency management director was concerned about one of the holes: "It looks ugly down in there. I can't tell how deep it is."[2] He advised residents to stay away from the subsidence area and instructed the Borough Council to fence it off, but local officials, unable to find sufficient fencing, put up a rope barrier instead. The rope was untied within a day or two, and no further efforts were made to cordon off the area. Within a week, two more cave-ins occurred in the borough.

In early June, two months after the interim report, the Office of Surface Mining reported that in the previous four months the fire had spread under an area of approximately three acres. Even many residents on the north end of town believed the problem was approaching emergency proportions. A middle-aged woman living there acknowledged in late April that she and several of her neighbors were about to request that gas monitors be installed in their homes. "If you'd have asked me a few months ago if I thought this fire was a real danger to the town," she reflected, "I would have said 'I don't know. I hope not.' But I know it's serious now, for everybody."

As the fire advanced into the borough and surrounding areas, legislators chastised the technical agencies for unnecessary delay in responding to the blaze. A state representative who chaired the House Mines and Energy Management Committee, citing the millions of dollars spent on flood relief in Johnstown, Pennsylvania, compared the mine fire to the 1889 Johnstown flood: "So what's the difference between a flood tragedy and a mine fire? . . . Something has to be done and I can assure you that our committee cares." A member of the federal House Interior Appropriations Committee, after visiting Centralia, described the fire as "worse than I thought."

Despite expressions of concern from elected officials, however, government agencies were slow to respond. In late March the Pennsylvania Department of Health complained that the DER was slow in turning over tapes collected from gas monitors in homes. An administrator from the health department publicly challenged the DER to "get a better handle on gas monitoring practices."[3]

Even before the public, agency representatives showed little concern for the residents' plight. At one public gathering, a young mother told neighbors and government officials of her family's unexplained headaches and dizziness, which had occurred only after a borehole was drilled near their home. The woman was convinced that drilling the borehole had shunted gases into her basement—hardly a new concern. Officials had in fact suggested on other occasions that this might be a problem for some residents near the drilling sites. On this occasion, however, the DER representative immediately put the woman on the defensive: "It's probably something in your home. I wouldn't jump to any conclusions that it is the mine fire." It was only a matter of weeks before the health department offered temporary housing to the family living next door to the woman, because of consistently high gas readings in their home.

This was hardly the only public discreditation of citizens' attempts to interpret the effects of the fire. On one telling occasion, a retired miner suggested to DER officials that he and other miners might help: "I have walked underneath this town. I can tell you where the pillars are and where they've been robbed. Doesn't it make sense to talk with me and others who worked in the mines? We might have some ideas on how to put this fire out." A DER official assured him that government engineers were doing everything possible to abate or extinguish the fire. "I do, however, appreciate your concern," the official conceded. Failure to legitimate this retired miner's claim to know something relevant to the problem was humiliating for him, and several minutes later he walked out of the meeting.

Not only condescension but confusion was often the result of official reports on technical aspects of the fire. When one official reported to the community that SO_2 monitoring had revealed no appreciable increase of this noxious gas in ambient air, a councilman asked why, if the readings were within normal limits, there was a heavy smell of sulfur on the south end of town. The official then admitted that the monitoring device was probably not altogether accurate. "If they can't pick it up, I suggest they get new equipment," the councilman said. The DER official did not respond.

In late May, the OSM announced that it would fund the digging of a trench to stop the southwest march of the fire. This disclosure pleased many residents who viewed it as the government's first concrete step to address the crisis. A week later, the OSM announced that it was no longer certain the trench was needed. Shortly after this announcement, the OSM declined to discuss the trench idea further.

In other words, the state and federal governments' response to the fire was no less confused and disorganized than the community's. Incapable of improvising when faced with a chronic technological disaster, both these levels of government only muddled along, blaming one another and the victims themselves for their incapacity to act.

In the meantime, the CCHD continued to work on its internal organization. The CCHD did not intend to engage in direct action to mitigate the hazards associated with the fire, because the group had concluded that the climate of social hatred was taking a heavier toll on the community than the gases or subsidences. Not being committed to a particular interpretation of the fire, the CCHD had considerable time to work on itself as a group. At meetings, members were to suppress their individual views about the technical dimensions of the mine fire and instead to cooperate in providing various services to the community. Each member volunteered to accomplish something concrete each week, even if it was only making a telephone call, then report progress on that specific task to the group at large and listen to its collective opinion. Physical sharing was also encouraged within the group. At the close of a meeting, members would frequently hug one another. The group would also gather periodically with their families to enjoy one-day retreats, to learn that they could play as well as work cooperatively. Having worked for over three months on its internal organization, the group decided it was time to hold its first community meeting. The goal was to show Centralians "that it was possible to meet in an orderly fashion, listen to one another, accomplish concrete business and adjourn. In short, we have to show folks in this town that meetings can work."[4]

The strategies to accomplish this purpose were based on members' perceptions of problems in conventional mine fire meetings. To avoid disorganization, each person attending the CCHD meeting would receive a copy of an agenda that would be followed closely, with an eye to a two-hour time limit. All would be welcomed and introduced to the rules for group discussion by which CCHD normally operated. Each member of CCHD was to describe some facet of the group's activities—an overview of the CCHD organization, say, or the objectives of the group and its accomplishments to date. In addition to presenting itself as a model for communal action, the CCHD intended to position itself publicly as a group that was not going to interpret the fire. It would serve as mediator by offering residents a neutral ground for a meeting place, by interpreting each side's position to the other, and by communicating in the context of a public occasion the optimistic attitude that compromise was possible.

Although the CCHD's first public meeting on March 29, 1983, had been advertised in the newspaper and on the radio, only twenty residents attended, most of whom lived in the impact zone. If the group was to provide the basis for the communal reconstitution of the village it knew it must reach more than twenty people per meeting.

At the CCHD's next public meeting, a month later, people were asked to write on a card three personal concerns about the fire and the future of the town and to read aloud the first concern written on their cards. The concerns were then listed on sheets of newsprint taped to the wall. This "group memory" served to orient discussion and permitted all to participate, as the goal of this meeting was to show participants that an orderly exchange of ideas was possible. Many residents commented on the meeting as quite an unusual social occasion. One man said it was the first meeting he had attended in years where "no one was shouted down." A woman observed that it was the first mine fire meeting at which she had entered the discussion.

The CCHD had succeeded at cooperative activity, but its agenda would work only if it could convince its neighbors that fighting over the technical details of the fire ensured an endless cycle of discord. At that, the CCHD was failing. Indeed, the members admitted to one another that they were able to disengage themselves from their emotive interpretations of the fire only while working with the group. After the second meeting, it was clear to the CCHD that it would have to address residents by entertaining, not changing, their interpretations of the crisis.

The divisiveness and the low attendance—twenty residents at the first meeting and only thirty-five at the second—were only symptoms of the severe social fragmentation among Centralia's population of only nine hundred. The mine fire was indeed a multidimensional reality in Centralia, institutionalized in several competing groups by early 1983: the CCHD, the Borough Council's Mine Fire Task Force, the Unity Committee, the Citizens to Save Byrnesville, and the remnant of the Concerned Citizens. Other, informal groups were also springing up to represent conflicting interpretations of the crisis. One of these emerged from the ashes of the Unity Committee: the Residents to Save the Borough of Centralia, which advocated a position fundamentally opposed to that of the CC.

The Borough Council was chiefly concerned with maintaining community order and ensuring that it remained the principal authority in town. The Citizens to Save Byrnesville interpreted the mine fire as a threat to their particular neighborhood. The Unity Committee had come to support the cold-side understanding of the crisis as manageable, if only government could be prompted to act. The Residents to Save the Borough represented a more radical interpretation of the problem than its parent group, the Unity Committee. The CC members, as we know, continued to view the problem as an immediate threat to their health and safety.

Divergent though they were, the groups had a common style

of coping—blaming other groups for the misery besetting the town. The CC blamed the government, the "unconcerned citizens," and the CCHD (for succeeding it while being inconsistent with the CC's goals). The Borough Council blamed the CC and the CCHD for challenging its rightful role of political leadership. The council also accused the groups of disregarding the residents who did not find the fire threatening. The Citizens to Save the Borough accused the CC and the CCHD of destroying the peace and tranquility of the old Centralia in the name of personal gain. Unity Committee members accused the CC of selfishness that threatened their way of life. This pattern of coping with the environmental crisis by holding others morally culpable created a degree of social stress more severe than the stress of the fire itself.

The CCHD found it impossible to function in a mediating role amidst this whirlwind of competing groups. An additional obstacle the CCHD confronted in its effort to become a model for communal association was a haphazard and ineffective pattern of interaction common to the groups. Although each of the groups subscribed to a different interpretation of the crisis, all functioned in the same manner. Participants interrupted one another at meetings, which had no agendas; issues debated were left unresolved; leadership was a shifting, competitive proposition; and unrealistic goals were all too frequently pursued. It was the factious, conflict-ridden CC, rather than CCHD, that served these successor groups as a model for collective action.

Frustrated by low attendance at its initial meetings, the CCHD quite unwittingly sacrificed its goal of mediating the conflicting interpretations for the shorter-term goal of bigger turnouts at a series of meetings, each one targeted at a specific area of town. Approximately fifty residents attended the first meeting, most of them residents of the impact zone, but at least forty of them new to CCHD workshops. The CCHD was beginning to reach the community. The meeting contrasted sharply with the typical Centralia gathering. As people walked in, they were given a meeting agenda, which included a statement of purpose and guidelines for workshop behavior; 3-by-5 cards were handed out on which participants were to answer the question, "What do you want as residents living in the impact zone?" Thirty-one of the forty-one people who turned in a card expressed a desire to relocate.

The discussion then shifted to what resources were available to impact zone residents to work toward their goal of relocation. Led by several former CC members, the discussion identified legal help as the first resource available. The group decided that it was time to contact a Washington law firm that had worked previously with the CC. With collective enthusiasm the group adopted a suggestion that impact zone residents take their concerns immediately to the Borough Council. Residents were to request a public meeting with the council to tell their local political representatives what the group wanted. "What should we say to Council, exactly?" asked one man. "We're going to tell them," answered another, "that we, the residents of the impact zone, will make decisions from now on about what should be done about what we want." A round of applause followed. The chairman of the CCHD, sensing a confrontation in the making, reminded the residents to "approach Borough Council respectfully!"[5]

The meeting had accomplished what CCHD had set out to do; it provided a structure for collective decision making. At the same time, the CCHD had unwittingly created an occasion for residents holding one interpretation of the fire to reinforce their beliefs and seek an immediate resolution to their predicament. Trouble started the day after the workshop meeting, when word spread quickly around town that residents from the impact zone were planning a showdown with Borough Council. The council, in fact, simply ignored the CCHD's request for a special meeting. It was not inclined to a confrontation, and it had other concerns to pursue.

In the meantime, several impact zone inhabitants circulated

a petition among their neighbors on the hot side of town. Sixty-
seven people signed the petition, later known as the Citizens
Proclamation. It read:

For more years than we care to remember, we affected citizens have
remained mute over many issues as related to the Centralia Mine
Fire, and its silent aftermath, gases . . . we residents will no longer
accept being treated as second class citizens. . . . The will of the
people should be respected and honored. It is about time the horse
is placed in front of the cart, instead of vice versa. Our four priority
points are:
    Those who wish to be removed from the impact zone be given
the opportunity and resources to do so.
    We request, those who are relocated, be given fair market value
for their respective properties.
    We request the fire itself be addressed, other than occasional lip
service.
    Regardless of peoples' course of actions, their decision is theirs,
and as such, must be respected.

A CCHD member whose wife had circulated the petition
requested at the CCHD's weekly meeting that the organization
sponsor it. The group debated the idea and decided to remain
neutral, given the obvious conflict already generated by the petition and the proposed meeting with the Borough Council. The
word "proclamation" was troublesome for the CCHD's chairman,
who reminded the group that to proclaim something is not to
seek a communal basis for cooperative action. A proclamation is
a tactic that confronts others with a foregone conclusion, demanding compliance instead of requesting cooperation.
    On May 26, 1983, the Borough Council held a special meeting
to discuss the possibility of hiring an independent engineering
firm to provide a "second opinion as to data on the mine fire."[7]
During a lull in the discussion, the CCHD member who had
championed the petition stood and announced that he was not
speaking as a member of any group, but as a resident of the

impact zone. Several council members, anticipating what was coming, tried to ignore him and continued their discussion of the independent engineer. He was not to be ignored, however, and started reading the "Citizens Proclamation." Immediately after the proclamation was read, the council minutes report, "A motion to adjourn . . . was made." The motion did not carry and was followed by a motion that the council back the proclamation.[8] A heated debate ensued between members of the council and residents of the impact zone. Threats and counter-threats were exchanged, tempers mounted, and several councilmen walked out of the meeting before adjournment. The CCHD's plans to organize the town around a model for communal action were not working.

Several members of the embattled Borough Council blamed the CCHD for creating a public occasion designed to embarrass them, assuming that the proclamation originated with the CCHD and was a personal attack on the council. Many residents on the hill, however, counted the reading of the decree as a significant victory. Enjoying the council's obvious anger and annoyance at being forced to listen to and debate their demands, one woman crowed, "We got them right where it hurts, in front of the press and everybody."

The CCHD's model of cooperative conflict resolution was meeting stiff, if not insurmountable, opposition. In fact, at this juncture in the history of the town's efforts to cope with both the fire and the emerging norm of social hatred, none of the groups was succeeding. The pattern of group failure suggests that once set in motion, the tyranny of the town's social hatred precluded any self-conscious effort to rearrange the tragic pattern of interpersonal relations.[9]

The fire, however, was making progress. An Associated Press release, printed in the local paper on June 2, announced that the fire was moving and that gas samples from boreholes revealed "concentrations of carbon monoxide, carbon dioxide and methane that [are] hundreds and thousands of times above normal."[10]

Not only was the fire becoming of concern to more and more

residents of the borough but cold-siders were being told "unofficially" that the underground water table separating the south from the north end of town was not as high as first thought. Tunnels that had originally been thought to be under water were now believed to be above the water line and dry. In other words, there was no wall of water to stop the fire's advance into the north end of town. On June 14, the OSM officially announced that several tunnels leading from the south to the north end of town were indeed above the water line and quite capable of carrying the fire to the cold side of Centralia.[11]

On June 8, only a week before the announcement, approximately forty residents from the north side of town had attended the CCHD's second workshop, organized like the first. At the door, residents were given a meeting agenda stating that "index cards will be handed out, and everyone will write three responses to the . . . question: In terms of Centralia as a community, what do you want?"[12]

The results were surprising, in that twenty-four of the thirty-seven cold-siders who filled out a card listed relocation as their primary need. It would appear, then, that by early June 1983, Centralians were becoming aware that the mine fire posed a greater threat to their well-being than had been imagined. For some who wanted to relocate, concerns over health and safety were paramount. For others, it was not gases or subsidence that threatened their sense of security, but the confusion and misunderstanding perpetuated by the twenty-one-year-old fire. For many Centralians, the quality of life had so deteriorated that relocating to another community was viewed as problem-solving behavior.

No matter what individual conclusions had been reached about relocation, the results of the government-sponsored study on the fire marked the beginning of the end for Centralia. On July 12, the OSM made public the long-awaited conclusions of its study of the boundaries of the mine fire, along with the various options to abate or extinguish it. In an unusual display of media understatement, the local paper announced, "Mine fire news not good." In its "Engineering Analysis," GAI Consultants, the engineering firm that had conducted the study, reported that there was not one fire but many: "The Centralia mine fire is not a single . . . entity . . . advancing through the coal field on a broad, uniform front. Instead, the fire is composed of somewhat ill-defined, irregularly shaped zones of combustion."[13]

The report identified four separate fires, or "zones of combustion," which were moving in both southerly and northerly directions. The fires "could conceivably burn beneath the northern portion of Centralia" and would most definitely move under the borough of Byrnesville. Indeed, the fires were moving in the general direction of several contiguous communities and "could conceivably spread over an area of approximately 3,700 acres," roughly six square miles. The report noted that anthracite mine fires are extremely difficult to control and, if left to burn themselves out, might last for "a century or more." The study recommended total excavation as the only proven method for extinguishing an anthracite mine fire, estimating that in Centralia's case the cost would exceed $663 million. Short of that, four trenches could be dug in strategic places to stop the advance of the fire, at a cost of more than $120 million—no small sum, but only one-fifth the cost of total excavation.

The main trench of the four would cut a swath 3900 feet long, 450 feet deep, and an undetermined number of yards across. Because the trench must be dug ahead of the fire, the report warned that selecting this option meant digging a monstrous pit through the "heart of Centralia," shoveling out an estimated 9 million cubic yards of earth. Not only would this mean relocation for more than one hundred families and most of Centralia's businesses, but even the families that remained would have to resign themselves to "noise, vibrations [from blasting], dirt . . . [that] could continue for a period of several years." In fact, a spokesman for the engineering consultants estimated that such a large trench would take approximately thirty-six months to complete—if "shifts working twenty-four hours a day, seven days a week encountered no major obstacles" in the course of their work. "In view of these factors," the consultants wrote, "the relocation of households and businesses in response to local conditions brought about by the fire would appear to be a course of action worthy of consideration."

The engineers also candidly observed that despite the appreciable monetary, human, and environmental costs of the trenching options, "the success of the fire control measure is not necessarily assured." The report went on to mention other engineering options—bulk filling of mine workings beneath the community, inert gas injection, and incremental flooding—but cautioned against these techniques as being even more experimental and less predictable than either trenching or excavation.

The magnitude of the problem reported by the engineering firm prompted one politician to comment shortly after the report was made public: "The world changed as of this morning. . . . The potential area of risk is so much greater than we thought it was."[14] Government agency officials, legislators, and the media lost no time in reminding Centralians that the report was, in the words of a retired state official, "the town's marching orders." An OSM official, addressing almost two hundred Centralians on the day the report was made public, minced no words: "It has taken twenty-one years to get to this point; your job now is to tell us what you want. It is your decision, you tell us what you want. But you must tell us quickly."

Many Centralians hoped that an independent expert opinion would help them interpret the results of the borehole study and make a rational decision, but this was not to be the case. Several weeks before the government's engineering study was made public, the CCHD had offered $2,500 to the local government for hiring an independent engineer to give a second opinion. The Borough Council wrote the CCHD that it was about to solicit bids for just that purpose, and "CCHD's contribution would be greatly appreciated."[15] The CCHD replied to the Council that a "contract must be signed with Council as to our contribution to the expense of hiring an engineer, and the information we must receive. This information must be equivalent to the information which Council receives."[16]

The council did not respond to the CCHD's letter requesting a contract; in the words of one councilman, "We're the elected authority in the town. Why do we have to sign contracts with people from our own town?" At a public meeting in late June, when the council announced that it had hired an independent engineering firm, CCHD members' questions about access to workshops to discuss the engineers' report went unanswered. The council president told CCHD members, "When the final report is released, you'll get a copy at the same time as everybody else," including the Unity Committee and Columbia County, which had also contributed to the engineering fund. "As far as I'm concerned, someone who gives $5 is the same as you."

Angry at the council's disregard for the size of its pledge, the CCHD withdrew its offer and hired its own independent engineer. Because the small village could not agree on how technical information should be shared, its representatives paid almost $10,000 dollars to purchase two independent engineering evaluations of the same government-sponsored data. As it turned out, the two reports on the federal government's data differed sharply.

The Borough Council's engineering report supported the federally sponsored study in recommending total relocation as the only indisputable assurance of safety.[17] Residents living in fear of the fire found reason to smile at the "cold-side" council's having paid for a study that supported the threat beliefs of hot-side residents. On the other hand, the CCHD's engineers saw a possibility that Centralia might make a profit from its disaster, by "controlling the fire, and thereby the gas emissions," which would "eliminate all the current haphazard venting." In a paper submitted to the CCHD, "A Concept to Convert the Central Mine Fire from a Perceived Hazard to an Asset,"[18] the firm recommended that it be hired to implement a "controlled burn-out" that would save the town and bring huge revenues from the sale of thermal energy to local utilities.

Rumors of this report circulated in Centralia to the delight of many cold-side residents, who enjoyed the idea that the CCHD had spent the CC's grant money to be told that the fire was not a disaster at all, but the economic salvation of the borough. In the meantime, the CCHD reminded the engineers that they were being paid to analyze the government's data and not create work for themselves. The firm finally submitted a report that recommended further research before adopting any engineering option.[19] Many hot-side residents charged the CCHD with poor judgment in hiring that firm.

Like most of Centralia's futile attempts to gain some control over its destiny, this duplication of function and waste of money for second opinions generated only conflicting information. Confusion reigned over the summer, as the factions in Centralia struggled to expand their influence and out-position one another.

Preparing for the release of the GAI report, the Borough Council asked several citizens to form a committee to explore ways of giving residents an opportunity to respond to the report's recommendations.[20] This was the origin of the Centralia Input Task Force, the fifth group to be formed in two years and the fourth in eight months. It was the shortest-lived of the five groups, holding only three meetings. Perhaps its only contribution of note was initiating what would later be called Neighborhood Area Meetings, although the group itself fell apart before the meetings even started, the victim of misunderstanding between the CCHD and the council.

Because a consultant for the CCHD sat on the task force, the CCHD had assumed that the task force represented a joint effort with the council. This quickly proved to be an erroneous assumption. On July 9, the CCHD told the press that "a series of meetings at which Centralia and Byrnesville citizens can learn about and discuss the options . . . for dealing with the 21-year-old mine fire" were being planned.[21] The next day, the council corrected the CCHD by calling the press to announce that "Borough Council, not Centralia Committee For Human Development, will sponsor the meet-and-discuss sessions."[22]

Contrasting the successful target workshops that had been sponsored by the CCHD with the acrimonious gatherings sponsored by the council, many residents called council members to urge that the CCHD be given the lead role in organizing the Neighborhood Area Meetings. Rather than compete with the CCHD for the trust of the community, the council cancelled the "meet-and-discuss session." On July 15, a few days after the federal government released its report on the fire, the Borough Council held a public meeting that attracted fewer than forty people, who spent most of the time questioning the council's decision to cancel the neighborhood gatherings. A follow-up gathering on July 19 attracted even fewer people and prompted one concerned state legislator to chastise the group. "I really wish," he said loudly, "you would get together and decide on the most feasible option and spend less time quibbling and nitpicking." Given the council's poor track record at organizing and conducting public meetings, the CCHD announced on July 22 that it would sponsor the "Neighborhood Area Meetings."

Thus, in a matter of only a few days, a new group emerged and dissolved; meetings were planned, announced, canceled, and rescheduled; and the meetings that in fact took place did little more than add to the tarnish on the image of Borough Council.

A few days after the CCHD pledged to take over the local sessions, Borough Council made a last-ditch effort to take control by announcing a plan that it had drawn up for assisting residents in making their individual decisions to stay in Centralia or relocate. Rather than making a community decision and forcing government to be accountable to the collective, the council addressed the community as a group of individual interests, expressing the radical subjectivity typical of this embattled community: "Every homeowner in the borough of Centralia . . . is [to be] approached by a government official and asked whether or not they would like to relocate or remain in our community. . . . If any person feels he or she needs more information to make their final decision they should feel free to contact any member of . . . Council."[23]

The president of the council expressed a profound pessimism that his community could reach any kind of consensus regarding its collective destiny: "The position we took is really giving everyone the chance to communicate one to one what they would like to have done. . . . What it leaves as a solution to the fire is that it gives each individual a choice as to what they would like to have done."

As it turned out, the council's attempt to satisfy everyone actually won favor with no one. A hot-side resident questioned the wisdom of the council's approach: "You've gone ahead and chosen and took a position without first hearing from everyone in the community." Others pointed out that once again Borough Council has failed at leadership in moving toward a collective decision, choosing only to poll individuals again and record their opinions. The council's decision, in effect, was not to decide.

In the meantime, the CCHD was organizing the Neighborhood Area Meetings, five gatherings held simultaneously at various neighborhood locations throughout the borough. The meetings were an offshoot of a sociological survey of the community that showed Centralians to be strongly attached to their neighborhoods—in fact, more strongly attached to their neighborhoods than to their community. The structure of the sessions was modeled on the successful meetings that the CCHD had conducted in the past. The objective was to "give the citizenry access to a convenient and nonthreatening context within which they can express their opinions and listen to the opinions of their neighbors."

More than two hundred residents attended the five sessions, held on the evening of July 26. Citizens who were absent were asked for their opinions in a door-to-door survey conducted the following day. More than three hundred residents participated in the CCHD's efforts to give voice to citizens' preferences regarding the future of their town. Seventy-three percent of those attending the meeting or responding to the survey expressed the desire to relocate. In a survey of Centralia businesses done concurrently with the Neighborhood Area Meetings, 90 percent of the eighteen proprietors in town favored relocation. When a state legislator from the area learned the survey results, he made reference to euthanasia. "I guess," he mused, "they pulled the plug on that community."

The consensus of a majority of residents in favor of leaving town was, of course, the ultimate irony in the Centralia story. Solidarity was reached on the one solution that assured the death of the town: a majority of residents wanted out. This hard-won consensus expressed itself in the formation of yet another group, the Centralia Homeowners Association, which would lobby for the rights of individual Centralians amidst the bureaucratic entanglements of a federally sponsored relocation program. It would be this group, which facilitated the death of the town, that would attract more members than any previous group in the tumultuous history of this northern Appalachian village.

8. "This Town Is Dead"

Although the Neighborhood Area Meetings on July 26 produced a consensus on the future of Centralians, the mayor and the Borough Council refused on the next evening to recognize the citizens' plebiscite favoring relocation. The refusal was based not on the results of the meetings, but on who had sponsored them. As one councilman made very clear, "We are the elected officials responsible for this town, not anybody else."

The mayor opened the public meeting on July 27 by calling the neighborhood meetings "nonsense." "What do we need this for?" he yelled. Some people in the audience shouted back at the mayor, the noise level rose, and at one point two citizens started to climb over the table at which the council was seated, apparently ready for a fist fight. Someone from the audience yelled, "Enough! End this meeting!" In a rare moment of agreement, another responded, "Yeah, I'm going home—this town is dead." Nothing more was said, and people started drifting out of the building.

At this point, state agencies took a hand in prodding the Borough Council to act responsibly. Officials from the Department of Environmental Resources and the Department of Community Affairs, pressured the council to conduct a referendum on the question of relocation. Of the 545 votes cast in Centralia on August 11, 345 favored relocation, while two hundred voters wanted to remain in Centralia.

In the opinion of the Office of Surface Mining, the almost two-to-one vote in favor of relocation was "probably a wise option," since "like it or not, all Centralians would probably have to be relocated." There is evidence to suggest that the federal and state governments were sufficiently impressed by the engineering report on the magnitude of the Centralia mine fire to have concluded on their own that the town must go. Several days

before the August 11 referendum, the Pennsylvania Department
of Health whose director had only months earlier denied that
any danger existed in Centralia, distributed throughout town a
two-page report, "Health Related Problems Associated with
Trenching and Excavating." The report paints a vivid picture.
Noting that dynamite would be used regularly to blast through
the rock, the report warned that "Extremely high levels of noise,
particularly over a prolonged period of time, can damage the
nerves of the ear causing temporary and/or permanent loss of
hearing." On the question of particulate matter, the Health Department advised: "The excessive dust levels from digging and
blasting could irritate the throats and lungs of all residents.
Sneezing, coughing, and excessive nasal and throat mucous could
result."

The report continued by describing the dangers of subsidences
and the poisonous gases released into the air when burning coal
was brought to the surface. The final warning of the two-page
report is, from our perspective, most indicative of how distant
health officials were from the critical issues facing Centralians:
"Paramount among the other factors is a concern for the impact
of stress on the residents. . . . Some potentially stressful events
in Centralia [as a result of trenching or excavation] may be . . .
noise, questions of safety . . . and developing health problems."[1]

We can assume from this passage that the Department of
Health did not notice the extreme social disharmony in Centralia,
which was causing stress even greater than expected from trenching. The health department specialized in the use of sophisticated
instrumentation to identify and measure the indicators of disease
and injury caused by natural or technological agents, not the
signs of a breakdown in the social order.

The health department's report was only of consequence if a
decision was made to relocate the town, and by all accounts, the
government had made such a decision well in advance of the
August 11 referendum. Centralians had no choice in the matter,
as was made blatantly clear during the first week in August, when

the neighboring village of Byrnesville held its own informal referendum. At a public meeting that included officials from the OSM and the DER, a spokesman for Byrnesville stood up and announced that the residents had voted to remain in their homes and asked that the government implement a plan to stop the fire. The village had acted as it had been instructed by the state government, promptly and decisively. Byrnesville's decision, however, was obviously not what the government wanted to hear. A DER official took the floor following Byrnesville's announcement and said forcefully, "You made the wrong decision. Go back and think about it."

The August 11 referendum in Centralia was not the first chance for residents to express their views about relocation. Between 1981 and 1983, in no fewer than five polls sponsored by various organizations, Centralians consistently favored relocation by about a two-to-one margin. Before the summer of 1983, the state and federal governments' main response had been that the margin was not large enough to truly show what Centralians wanted. What apparently changed the government's position was the GAI engineering report, after which the two-to-one margin in the August referendum was reinterpreted as a clear majority favoring relocation, hence a mandate for the government to act.

And act the government did, with a swiftness all the more staggering in light of the two previous decades of indecisiveness and inconsistency. By the end of August, a little over a month after the release of the GAI report, DER and Columbia County Redevelopment Authority personnel were doing their own survey of Centralia residents to estimate costs of relocation. They were also researching the housing market within a twenty-mile radius of the borough.[2]

Lawmakers and agency officials were quick to embrace the relocation option. In mid-September, the two U.S. senators from Pennsylvania jointly wrote to Governor Thornburgh, urging that a relocation plan like the one at Love Canal be adopted.[3] Shortly thereafter, Interior Secretary Watt and Governor Thornburgh held a meeting after which Thornburgh reported: "The Secretary assured us that if we could justify expenditures, the funds would be forthcoming." Watt and Thornburgh would jointly chair an interagency task force to determine the cost of a government buyout.[4]

Less than two weeks later, proposed federal legislation for a $42-million appropriation to buy Centralia properties was approved by the House Appropriations Committee and sent on to the full House. The government would pay the fair market value of the property of owners who elected to sell, with no regard for the existence of the mine fire. The money would come from the OSM's Abandoned Mine Reclamation Fund, financed by active coal companies. Seventy-five percent would come from the Interior Department's share of the fund and the remainder from Pennsylvania's allotment.[5]

In early October, the appropriations bill came before the full House. A last-minute roadblock was removed by deleting money for a project unrelated to Centralia, to be considered separately at a later time. Ironically, from the perspective of technological hazards, the unrelated project was the Clinch River breeder reactor.

The $42 million appropriation made it through the House and Senate by November 18, only fourteen weeks after the date on which the government-sponsored engineering study was made public.

Although the government had finally acted to cope with potential risks to health and safety, no money was committed to do anything about the fire itself. The government's engineering study had recommended containing the fire by trenching. If this option were pursued, Centralians were told, blasting, dust, noise, and the like would make life in the borough intolerable. Many decided to relocate on the assumption that trenching would become a reality. But no commitment had been made.

This fact was not lost on some Centralians at the time. While supporting the $42-million buyout plan, the president of the newly-formed Centralia Homeowners' Association emphasized that the question of containment had not been answered: "We want the government to go to the heart of the problem and go after the fire."[6] Centralia's congressman expressed concern over a letter from the Federal Emergency Management Agency stating that the Interior Department would support either relocation or suppression of the fire, but not both. The concern about stopping the fire appears to have been well-founded: at this writing, there is no further government commitment to any method of containing or extinguishing the fire.

In any case, by acting decisively on relocation, the government made way for what would become the most successful grassroots organization in the history of Centralia: the Centralia Homeowners' Association.

The CCHD, though unable to redefine the terms of the conflict and create communal bonds, had convinced many in town that orderly meetings, at least, were possible. After the Neighborhood Area Meetings in July of 1983, the CCHD, at the request of several residents, agreed to help organize a group to represent individual homeowners in negotiating with the government for relocation subsides, as well as those residents who chose to stay in town. The first meeting, on August 16, attracted more than one hundred homeowners, most of whom favored relocation.

In the months to come, the Centralia Homeowners' Association would attract a membership of over three hundred, making it the largest grasroots group in the history of the borough. Adopting the CCHD's model for public meetings, the Homeowners' became a well-organized group representing the needs of a majority of Centralians. But, the Homeowners' was not intended to fill the needs of the community of Centralia for close bonds of identification, but to serve the pecuniary interests of individuals. Ironically, the reason for joining the group was the recognition that joint action was the most efficient means of meeting individual needs. "I'm a member of Homeowners'," revealed one man, "because the government will take me to the cleaners if I let them. I figure for $5 bucks a year [the membership fee], I'll join if it will help me get the most [money for my home]."

Another man was more blunt: "Look, the government's out to screw me; I'll join anybody who helps me screw them instead."

As the following excerpt from its articles of incorporations suggests, the Homeowners' Association was the organized expression of a town where a majority opinion was possible only when the needs of the individual were paramount: "We the members of the Centralia Homeowners' Association join together in order to promote the future welfare of every homeowner and tenant in Centralia and to maximize any assistance forthcoming from state and federal governmental agencies concerning the homeowners and tenants of Centralia and the mine fire that threatens their homes."

Shortly after the Homeowners' organized, a seventh grassroots group emerged, like the final expression of a town unable to heal itself. Based on the long-standing model of blame attribution and confrontation, the Citizens to Save the Borough of Centralia waged a bitter campaign against those of their neighbors who had decided to relocate.

Organized by five or six families who would not accept the evidence that the entire borough was now at risk, the Citizens to Save the Borough grew to more than two dozen families, many of them elderly, who wanted to remain in town and who accused their neighbors of trying to "soak the government for a new house." The group appealed to a vision of Centralia that identified people with their houses, under a cultural idea of "homes": "Speak out and defend your homes—your little town of Centralia is in danger. When one speaks of 'home' they speak of something they love, even with all its imperfections and are reluctant to leave it without serious reasons. Some homes are identified with certain families, generation after generation, and are a source of pride and love to them. You do not destroy your home because it needs to be repaired and neither should Centralia be sacrificed because it has imperfections. . . . Do not be afraid, stand up and be counted for Centralia."[7]

Although the group spoke of the values of communality, the "SOBs" (Save Our Borough), as they were jokingly referred to by some Homeowners' Association members, held their meetings in secret, closed to any one who was not a member. The group's strategy, by now normative for Centralia, relied on blame attribution, disrupting public meetings, and accusing neighbors of "selling out" and abandoning the town.

But the group was at worst a minor annoyance for the majority of residents, who had decided to accept the government's offer to relocate. The Citizens to Save the Borough is significant, not in its achievements, but in underscoring the point that the real disaster in Centralia was above ground, not below it. Structurally similar to the groups that preceded it, the Citizens pursued the goal of communal solidarity by way of divisive action. The Homeowners' Association, by contrast, pursued the self-interest of each member by way of cooperative action. It appears that at this juncture in the town's history, personal pecuniary interest was the only motivation for engaging in the type of communal action that the CC, the Unity Committee, and other groups in town had sought.

In their rear guard action, the Citizens confirmed the extreme subjectivity of Centralians, which precluded any consensus on the "reality" of the mine fire in terms of their health and safety. The inherent ambiguity of the mine fire, distorted by the media and treated in a contradictory fashion by the government, gave rise to several competing interpretations of the same world, each of them supported by both sensory and official intelligence.

It is now the winter of 1987. There are about thirty families still living in Centralia. With the exception of a few households, the entire village of Byrnesville has been relocated. Over the course of the past four years, families have been relocating a few at a time and their houses have been razed. Many homes are boarded up, waiting to be torn down. These have been relatively peaceful years in Centralia. With the strength that comes when a final decision is made, families have quietly pursued their various options for relocating, some finding just what they need in the real estate listings, others building new homes, still others looking for older houses to fix up. Several families have moved to a new development, called informally "New Centralia," which lies only a few miles from their former town. With few exceptions, the families have moved to better houses; many now live in houses two to three times the size of their Centralia residences. The Homeowners' Association was successful in getting a senior citizens' residence built in a nearby town to accommodate the elderly in Centralia who chose not to buy another home.

Not surprisingly, a relocated family seldom, if ever, returns to Centralia, relieved that the days of anger and danger are over. Most, if not all, former Centralians interpret relocation as a positive life change. Some see it in terms of physical safety and better health, others in terms of relief from the stress of social conflict. For all, this is an opportunity to begin anew, without the threat of an underground ecological menace or an above-ground social disaster. As one homeowner put it, in response to the claim that the fire could be contained: "Maybe you're right. I just know that I got to move. I don't know how many years I have left. I'd like to spend them at peace with myself."

9. Making Sociological Sense of the Story

A funeral was held in Centralia recently. Black-clad middle-aged and elderly people entered coal-black limousines, which lined the curb in front of one of the few remaining occupied row homes on Locust Avenue. Burial was in the Odd Fellows' Cemetery on the hot side of town. Within sight of boarded-up homes and of steam spewing from the ground and from venting pipes rising toward the sky, the priest from a neighboring town said the committal prayers: " . . . we commit her body to the ground; earth to earth, ashes to ashes, dust to dust. The Lord bless her and keep her, the Lord make his face to shine upon her and be gracious to her, the Lord lift up his countenance upon her and give her peace."

The words echo as if intended for Centralia itself. No one in Centralia died because of the mine fire. But a community died, and with it much of the spirit of many proud and courageous people. This is no small loss; some would say hardly less than life itself.[1]

We have emphasized throughout this book that what befell Centralia was a social as well as an environmental disaster. From our perspective, it was the way people responded to one another that constituted the most profound disaster in Centralia. Yet the social breakdown reflected not the shortcomings of individuals, but rather the severe demands that a chronic technological disaster places on a social system.

There is a wide variance between the way communities respond to natural disasters and the way they respond to technological disasters. The altruistic community that emerges in the wake of a natural calamity contrasts sharply with the social hatred that characterized Centralians' response to their long-term, humanly produced disaster. Why does a natural disaster result in the communal bonding of survivors and a CTD tend toward debilitating social conflict? In this final section, we will modify several key concepts in natural disaster research and place them in a loosely defined theoretical schema to account for the variance in collective responses to CTDs and natural disasters. Our intention is to place the Centralia study within a broader comparative context that can serve as a guide to emergency response planners and to future researchers on the sociology of long-term humanly produced disasters.

"Community" can be defined as a structure of institutions located in space or as a specific type of human association. Our interest is in the effects of CTDs on primary human associations, those groups larger than the family, yet less complex and impersonal than corporations. Our concern is with groups that emphasize criteria of common belonging rather than pecuniary or instrumental criteria, associations that provide a person's most essential experiences of collective life outside the family. In particular, we are interested in the belief that the political boundaries of a municipality coincide with the symbolic boundaries of the primary associations, a belief common to small towns and villages.

A considerable body of research is available on the communal associations that spontaneously emerge in the aftermath of a natural disaster; the almost unselfconscious revitalization of community in the wake of natural destruction is a well-documented fact. Our research and that of others to be discussed here indicates that communal groups act very differently in the context of CTDs; communal bonds disintegrate and are replaced by emergent groups that compete for control of the crisis. We will show that this contrasting perspective may be of use to policy makers and sociologists interested in environmental issues and in the nature of conflict.

Another reason for focusing on an associational definition of community is the relative significance of such communal groups in the type of human settlements most likely to be the site of CTDs, namely working- or lower-class rural areas.

Natural disasters are not especially class-biased. While it is true that disasters most severely affect the lower classes, a tornado is just as likely to strike an upper-middle-class neighborhood as a lower-class area. Neither cities nor towns nor villages are spared the devastation of natural cataclysms, which strike human settlements of all sizes.

In sharp contrast, chronic technological disasters are very class-specific, being much more likely in areas where the population is largely working or lower class.[2] Because it is precisely those areas that lack extensive, formal economic and political resources with which to fight CTDs, they must rely mainly on primary communal associations to see them through. A recent study by the General Accounting Office found that four hazardous waste landfills in one state were located in communities where a majority of the population is black; at all four sites the black population in the surrounding census areas has a lower mean income than the mean income for all races combined.[3] Another study found that the city of Houston, Texas, pursued a policy of locating solid waste disposal sites in low-income, predominantly black neighborhoods.[4]

CTDs are less likely to occur in cities than in small towns, and particularly likely to occur in lower- or working-class towns that have historically depended on big corporations and extra-local governments, where the centers of power lie far from the settlement itself. Among the more well-known CTD occurrences are the dioxin contamination of Times Beach and several other small towns in Missouri; the asbestos contamination in Globe, Arizona; the Love Canal neighborhoods of Niagara Falls, New York; and, of course, Centralia.[5]

The severe disruption of a CTD presents more intractable problems for small towns than it would for large cities. Small towns cannot mobilize extensive governmental and social service machinery to respond effectively to a CTD. The smaller the locality, the more dependent residents become on both extra-local bureaucracies and their town's informal process and organizations to meet their collective needs and prompt government to act on their behalf. In the small town, the front line of attack on collective crises is mechanical solidarity—the bonds of communal association manifested in friendship groups, voluntary associations, and kin networks, and the shared belief that the boundaries of the town are but the physical expression of a common identity.

When a CTD occurs, the demands often overwhelm a town's communal associations. Local groups are called upon to do tasks for which they have inadequate resources, structures, and experiences. Groups that have related only on personal, informal terms are called upon to become more detached and efficient to represent the needs of residents struggling to protect their health and property. In taking on this chore, local groups are bound to please few residents. As the Centralia case clearly shows, the differential impact of the disaster agent causes neighbors to experience and interpret the same world, "our community," in very divergent ways. We would expect this situation to create a substantially heavier burden on primary groups that take responsibility for organizing the town.

What happens to a community's structure and its culture when confronted with a crisis? In a literature survey, Anthony Wallace suggested that in an "extreme situation," socially understood coping strategies are rendered ineffective, while at the same time the population experiences a "drastic increase in tensions, to the point of causing death or major personal and social readjustment."[6] Wallace emphasizes the concept of society as a structure positioned in space and time, a structure that is lost when aversive agents threaten life and property and disorganize the accepted patterns of crisis management. This idea of the extreme environment as a time between points of stability is found elsewhere in the literature on disasters.[7]

Implicit in Wallace's work, and in that of others, is the acceptance of the immediate-impact natural disaster as the classic aversive agent.[8] But it is reasonable to assume that the type of extreme environment and the specific manner in which the routine socio-emotional patterns of a community become unstructured are closely tied to the type of aversive agent besetting the society. To help distinguish between the two types of extreme environments—one natural and short-term, the other technological and long-term—consider the stages in the conventional model of natural disasters.

When natural disasters are the cause of extreme environments, the unstructuring of routines and common coping modes typically begins with the *warning stage*, the apprehension that a calamity may occur.[9] By the *threat state*, when there are unequivocal signs of the approaching disaster force, the extreme situation is under way. During impact, a maelstrom of flying debris or raging floods or towering walls of fire rip apart the last vestiges of "business as usual" in the full force of nature's wrath. The *impact stage* is temporally significant because it marks the most intense point in the disaster sequence, after which there may be considerable pain and grief but the destruction is over.

During the *inventory* and *rescue stages* immediately following impact, survivors begin to assess their losses and gradually piece together a picture of what has happened. Survivor groups emerge spontaneously—small, altruistic communities whose goals include treating the wounded, extinguishing fires, and freeing trapped victims. With the onset of the *remedy stage*, the extreme situation begins to subside as outside relief agencies take control of the disaster scene and impose a formal structure (not always with the approval of the survivors) on the inventory and rescue stages. During the *recovery stage*, the extreme environment is replaced with either a reconstitution of the old structure or a modified pattern of personal and collective life.

Note that in this stage model, the time lapse between the warning, threat, impact, and inventory and rescue stages may be very brief—in some cases, only several minutes. The period most likely to be extended in time is the warning stage. The eruption of Washington State's Mount St. Helen's volcano in

1980, for example, had been anticipated for several weeks. The time lapse between the threat stage and the inventory–rescue, however, was less than an hour. The extreme environment created by natural disasters is typically short-lived, a horrendous moment in time bounded by two periods of stability—one historical, the other emergent. The customary sequence of stages in a natural disaster moves a community from order, to chaos, to the reconstitution of order. At that point, the disaster enters the collective memory, recalled only on those occasions deemed appropriate for remembering a shared experience of horror.

The type of extreme environment created by a chronic technological disaster differs considerably from this description. The Centralia study and the work on Love Canal speak of a protracted, seemingly endless period of time between the discovery of the aversive agent and the realization that its worst consequences are past. There is no brief moment of terror, to be followed by an easily defined sequence of inventory, rescue, remedy, and recovery. Indeed, for many Centralians and residents of Love Canal, relief from fear came only when they were permanently removed from their homes and towns, a process that took several years.

CTDs tend to trap at least some of the population in the warning and threat stages of the model, freezing them in extended periods of apprehension and dread. A mine fire that moves slowly through accessible veins, or toxic chemicals that leach invisibly through underground swales, may at times give signals that danger is near, but the signals are frequently vague and open to dispute. Long-term exposure to warning and threat, particularly when distributed unevenly through the population, places severe demands on the coping resources of a settlement.

Occasionally, individuals or families feel the impact of the agent, in the form of subsidence, a chronic cough, or lassitude. But since the experience rarely extends beyond the person or the family, it is not likely to become the occasion for communal action. Indeed, the source of the threat—the reason that a family is always tired or a child or grandparent has upper respiratory trouble—is itself frequently vague to the point of inviting multiple interpretations. In other words, the impact of the CTD, to borrow a distinction from C.W. Mills, is more likely to remain a "trouble," a personal problem, than to become an "issue," a socially recognized occasion for communal response.[10]

Trapped by a CTD in the first two stages of the disaster cycle, a population is prevented from progressing to the point of reassembling itself into a complementary distribution of understandings and tasks. Any attempt at what we might call remedy and recovery are not humanistic efforts directed toward the affected population but technical activities aimed at disposing of the aversive agent. More likely than not, as we witnessed at Times Beach, Centralia, and Love Canal, remedial and recovery technology, however confounded by political game playing, will be unable to stop the advance of the disaster agent. Residents are rescued only by relocation, which does not allow the settlement to reestablish itself. The web of social positions woven by common understandings is ripped apart before there is an end to the severe social and ecological disruption.

The more the stages of warning and threat become institutionalized—that is, the more these normally temporary stages take on the character of permanence—the greater will be the toll on affected populations. A CTD does not create a moment between points of stability; rather, it imposes a fixed, seemingly permanent period of instability, a time within which conventional patterns of behavior no longer seem to work. Extended period of ambiguous warning and threat cues destabilize a human settlement by rearranging the traditional pattern of social relationships.

The ways in which this process differs from that of immediate-impact natural disasters are examined in Wallace's concept of "mazeway disintegration." Wallace developed this concept to link the study of disaster to the role of culture in personal and collective life. The "maze" he defines is the objective world rendered into subjective landmarks (my photo albums, my spouse, my house, my street, my friends, the policeman I see every day at the busy intersection, and so on). The moral and rational codes for moving through these landmarks are called the "way." Wallace suggests that we "fall in love with [our] maze[s] and our way[s] of running [them] because they are associated with every satisfaction [we] derive from life."[11] When our maze-way is destroyed, we act "as if a beloved object were dead."[12]

The extreme environment created by immediate-impact disasters destroys both a portion of the object-world (the maze) and the conventions and rules for using that world (the way). For a relatively brief time, survivors are thrown into a milieu where structured positions do not exist; the terror experienced is that of chaos. Survivors sense an immediate, undeniable imperative to begin work on reconstituting their culture if they are to live beyond this horrifying moment. The thread of life has become too tenuous for survivors to remain passive. This imperative to survive the moment is linked to the visible, tangible destruction of the maze, which creates a wide range of opportunities for participation in collective tasks. The tasks that survivors engage in are helping, altruistic endeavors that require people to work side by side, in unison, to save lives and property. Such tasks encourage the formation of communal associations, which function to reassert the power of the group over nature by reconstituting routines that reinvest daily life with a sense of permanence and predictability. If an aversive agent instead inhibits a population from progressing past the warning and threat stage, there are no opportunities for spontaneous displays of solidarity; there is no occasion for rescue but plenty of time for anxiety and social discord.

In a CTD, it is not the *maze* but the *way* that undergoes the most devastation. In many cases, the maze itself remains intact; it is the way of getting through the maze that is dismantled. Ambiguity arises when government agents use polysyllabic technical expressions to "explain" a situation to an audience; when newspapers and magazines focus on the worst-case scenarios; or when friends and neighbors exhibit states of anxiety and dread, which spread in a contagion-like fashion from person to person.

Compounding the equivocal and volatile warning and threat stages of CTDs is their unconventional status in the meaning system of most cultures. Few people relish the experience of a natural disaster, but most people are at least able to invoke a shared meaning system to make sense out of what has happened. CTDs, however, are too new a phenomenon to have become routinized in popular culture. People experience CTDs' extended periods of warnings and threats without the benefit of a coherent meaning to render the trauma comprehensible. "Just what are we facing here?" "Where is it coming from?" "Is it really dangerous?" "Who is responsible for starting it and abating it?" "What should I do?" "How should I behave toward this issue?" Myriad questions go unanswered by culture when one's "way" has been damaged by a long-term technological crisis.

On the basis of our Centralia study and the work done on Love Canal, we suggest that the more indeterminate the warning and threat stages of an extreme environment and the more they are extended in time, the more residents will turn to symbolic activity to ascertain the degree of danger they are facing. The extended duration of CTDs, combined with the high degree of ambiguity created by lack of sensory confirmation and frequently by contradictory technical assessments, ensure that people will attach meaning to any number of cues in an attempt to make sense out of their experiences with the aversive agent. In the symbolic interpretation of warning and threat signals, people seek out others whose interpretations are similar to their own, and such affiliative behaviors in turn are likely to produce groups that become, over time, institutionalized. At this point, any new warning or threat—however ambiguous—will be interpreted by members according to the shared appraisal of the group. In such circumstances, groups engage not in consensual activities, but conflict; they emphasize not unity, but divisions; and the result is not the rebuilding of a sense of community, but its demise.

In natural disasters, it is not warnings and threats but recovery needs that give rise to emergent groups; they engage in the rehabilitative response that follows the worst-point experience of the disaster cycle. In the context of CTDs, however, groups emerge and gain momentum during the protracted stages of warning and threat, before there is any visible destruction to respond to. These groups are not formed with the intent of saving others, mourning the loss of the mazeway, and beginning the process of rebuilding. Rather, they are motivated by apprehension, worry, fear, and anxiety, in the emotionally charged context of warning and threat.

Freud observed a critical and common characteristic of the reconstitution of order following a natural disaster—the therapeutic community: "One of the gratifying and exalting impressions which mankind can offer is when in the face of an elemental crisis, it forgets the discordancies of its civilization and all its internal difficulties and animosities, and recalls the great common task of preserving itself against the superior power of nature."[13]

A unique feature of this rehabilitative response is the unreflecting commitment that victims express to one another as members of a group that survived catastrophe, who participated in the same dramatic moment in history, which outsiders cannot be assumed to appreciate fully. Indeed, spontaneous collective action in the immediate aftermath of a natural disaster generally accounts for most of the significant rescue work required.[14] The spontaneity of such communal action is captured in Raphael's description of survivor response to calamity: "Rescue of others seems almost automatic, a basic human response, perhaps evolved for the survival of the group."[15] It is not necessary, however, to invoke evolutionary images to understand this unreflecting communality.

In the unselfconscious enactment of a therapeutic community in the aftermath of a natural disaster, communal associations play the key role in reconstituting the basis for a contractual society. Quarantelli and Dynes suggest that natural disasters are "consensus-type" crises. The extreme environment created by the natural disaster is a "dramatic event in the life history of the community." For the survivors, it is "our disaster."[16] The visible, undeniable destruction of life and property triggers a therapeutic response.

At another level, we can postulate the necessity for the emergence of communal solidarity in post-impact situations if we examine Turner's statement that "organic solidarity cannot replace mechanical solidarity. Instead, organic solidarity requires, in addition to the division of labor, an effective substructure of mechanical solidarity."[17]

Turner is arguing that the existential community, the community of sentiment, is a necessary if not sufficient condition for the constitution or reconstitution of a complementary task-oriented society. The severe disruption of corporate life requires a period of dramatic communal enactment "to recreate the continuing assurances upon which organic solidarity depends."[18]

Stressing the technical side of the CTD, Baum and colleagues observed that a "technological disaster is more likely to cause long-term uncertainty and consequent psychological effects than are natural disasters."[19] The ambiguity breeds uncertainty, which undermines the basis upon which a therapeutic community might be formed. As Lang and Lang argue, "When disaster threatens over a long period of time, the cohesive forces that hold a group together are subject to strain."[20] Or, as Barton noted in his classic work, chronic disasters "may gradually drain resources and lower aspirations so that the whole system moves toward a less satisfactory equilibrium, or towards collapse as a system."[21]

Not only do CTDs inhibit the reconstitution of order through therapeutic communities; they also work toward the breakdown of communal structures and sentiments that previously existed. What is destroyed or impaired is the "way," the common understandings, the unstated assumptions, that this neighborhood or settlement is a community.

Consider the observations on intramural conflict culled from other studies of long-term, human-caused disasters. For example, in their study of Love Canal, Fowlkes and Miller found that: "For the most part . . . families that believe the chemical migration was of limited seriousness do not so much marshal a body of evidence in support of their position as they discredit any and all claims that migration [was] widespread. They discredit those claims primarily by categorically discrediting the people who make them."[22]

In Kasperson and Pijawka's research on asbestos contamination in Globe, Arizona, they found "that the non-victimized community [developed] sharp resentment against the disaster victims."[23] Cuthbertson and Nigg agree with this finding, arguing that "conflictive, rather than consensual, adaptation develops following a technological disaster."[24]

It has been pointed out that conflict can facilitate the stable growth of a society.[25] In the latter stages of a natural disaster, conflict facilitates the restructuring of society by helping to realign group interests and sustain the competitive milieu necessary for an organic division of labor. The question in this phase of the disaster cycle is not whether the settlement should continue to exist, but how to distribute power and resources in the reconstitution of the social order. The type of conflict that is likely to emerge in the remedial and recovery stages of a natural disaster takes place within a consensual framework supported by the therapeutic groups that emerge during the inventory and rescue stages.

In a chronic technological disaster, however, conflict typically emerges when competing interpretations of warning and threat cues have become institutionalized in concrete groups; this type of conflict places the basic consensus of a society in question. We propose that CTDs create a condition in which a choice must be made between several competing interpretations of the warning and threat cues, each demanding to be credentialed as the correct view of the situation. One group interprets the warning and threat messages as signals of impending disaster. Another group interprets the messages as remote risks—a potential problem but certainly nothing to warrant the destruction of the settlement. One group charges another with pursuing goals inimical to its members' health and welfare. In turn, the accused group blames its accuser of seeking to destroy its members' traditional way of life by working for relocation. This process of reciprocal blame attribution escalates into a conflict that may, as in the case of Centralia, become more debilitating than the hazard agent itself.

A CTD can be expected to disrupt, or even destroy, the traditional patterns of interpersonal relationships and shared understandings that serve to anchor personal life in a social context. This form of disruption is more insidious and harder to repair than the destruction of a town's material culture. It is one thing to rebuild a house; it is quite another to heal the pain and anger felt when neighbors become enemies. In the aftermath of a natural disaster, the loss of material culture evokes an outpouring of aid and sympathy from the vertical structure, easing the burden of rebuilding. There is no such outpouring to ease the loss of communality in a long-term technological disaster. Indeed, as in the case of Centralia, legislators and others in authority may chastise the town for failing to demonstrate the "democracy of stress" we have come to expect from those experiencing crises.[26]

Disasters of whatever sort severely inhibit, perhaps destroy, the capacity of a community to function routinely. If enactments of emotional and intrinsic attachments are prerequisites to the reconstitution of an exchange-based community life, any dynamic that impedes them will seriously hamper a town in responding to its tragedy. When a crisis prevents a town from engaging in the dramaturgy of communal solidarity, concerted, instrumental action to rid the community of the aversive agent will be all but impossible. A succession of failed attempts to construct communal associations may leave citizens embittered and demoralized. In the end, losses attributable to the breakdown in the social order may outweigh the losses attending the environmental hazard itself.

Natural disasters have become less terrifying. This is not to say that the number of natural disasters has decreased in post-industrial societies; the frequency of hurricanes and tornadoes now is roughly the same as one hundred years ago. What has changed is our ability to adapt to these natural phenomena. Early warning detection technology and pre- and post-disaster emergency response policies have greatly reduced the number of fatalities and the amount of property damage, while increasing the chances for successful recovery, even revitalization.[27] It is doubtful that we will ever be capable of preventing natural disasters, but we are gaining the upper hand in reducing their destructive effects.

Ironically, just as we are learning to control the devastating effects of natural disasters, human-made disasters of extended duration hit us more frequently. It was recently pointed out that "the major burden of hazard management in developed societies has shifted from risks associated with natural processes to those arising from technological development and application."[28] Estimates of the late 1970s predicted that technological disasters would continue to multiply, taking their toll in financial, social, and human devastation.[29] In the ten years since those forecasts, we have witnessed an almost relentless chain of chronic technological disasters, and there is little reason to believe that we have seen the worst.

As illustrated in this book and in the studies of other CTDs, governments and social service agencies must respond to this new type of disaster without the benefit of coherent and integrated local, state, or federal policies.[30] Legislators and social service personnel, in turn, find little help from the social and behavioral sciences in constructing technological hazard and disaster management policies that are consistent with the community response to this new genre of calamity. "We know very little," Slovic has argued, "about the social psychological factors that determine public response to technological risk."[31] Kasperson and Pijawka agree, noting that "[our] knowledge of long-term impacts of technological disasters is scant."[32] Pointing out the gaps in social and behavioral research on chronic technological disasters, Kliman and colleagues argued: "Long-term, invisible disasters . . . will become even more prevalent, increasing the need for psychological and sociological understanding of the consequences."[33]

The need to come to grips with the social and psychological consequences of CTDs is made even more urgent by the little we do know about them. As a community, Centralia is not an isolated case of therapeutic intervention being rendered impotent by the ravages of a CTD. Of a similar community, Kliman and colleagues have written: "Our frustrating and saddening experience in consulting with the United Way agencies at Love Canal was that the murkiness and pessimism of the situation resulted in divisions among victims. . . . Effective community organization was nearly impossible in an atmosphere of hopelessness and misplaced conflict."[34]

In the closing pages of this book, we have offered a loosely organized theory to account for the devastation of chronic technological disasters in terms of community conflict and disorganization, which may, as in the case of Centralia, generate as much stress as the disaster agent itself. Our purpose was to outline and discuss a perspective that could guide researchers, policymakers, and social service personnel in exploring or dealing with CTDs. For our colleagues, we hope that this perspective will help generate specific hypotheses that can be tested against empirical reality. For policy implementers, we hope that a sensitivity to the *social* dynamics emergent during a CTD will help generate a rational, humane, and timely response to the problems that arise in such a calamity. For policymakers, we hope that a better understanding of the effects of CTDs will inspire policies that aid the victims and minimize the hazards of the technologies that cause CTDs in the first place.

For the victims of future CTDs, we hope that our research helps to avoid or ameliorate the destruction of the social bond, that critical yet fragile entity upon which our personal and communal life is based.

Appendix: Participatory Research in Centralia

"We need to know whom we help and whom we injure and damage, intentionally and unintentionally, so that we can figure out what we should be doing and not doing in behalf of a better society, however "better" may be defined."[1]

It was a chilly fall day in 1981 when we took our first trip to Centralia. A slow rain was falling as we drove to the south end of town and parked the car, and a gaseous stream from the venting pipes wafted over the hill just behind a row of homes. We approached a woman sweeping wet leaves from her sidewalk; she was sweeping the leaves more slowly than they were falling. It hardly seemed worth the effort. We introduced ourselves and commented that it appeared she was fighting a losing battle with the leaves. She smiled in agreement and explained that with fewer and fewer neighbors stopping by to visit her, she had little to do but sweep. It was a rather sad encounter, of a nature that would be repeated time and again. This was our first clue that something was happening in Centralia that had not been reported in the media, something that appeared to be inconsistent with research on disasters and the altruistic community.

Before we first saw Centralia, we had made the moral judgment that environmental disasters are "bad." People should not be exposed to the danger and misery of toxic waste contamination or underground mine fires. Little did we know at the time that the most devastating loss was the breakdown of ties to neighbor, friend, and family. Nor did we know that our research would become part of the problem itself, as well as of efforts to solve Centralia's crisis. To resolve the moral dilemma we faced in Centralia, we adopted a participatory research strategy.

Our first hurdle after committing ourselves to the study was to agree upon the unit of analysis. Would we study the local government's response to the problem, focusing on the political aspects of the crisis? Would we study family adjustment or maladjustment to the threat of the fire? We discussed several options, but the only one that made any real sense to us was to focus on the community. "Theories about disasters," Torry reminded us, "are inherently theories about communities, that is, community continuity and change."[2]

In the summer of 1982, we conducted a community survey of the entire adult population of Centralia. Questionnaires were returned by 368 adults, or 56.9 percent of the adult population. The survey instrument was designed to reveal opinions about the quality of life in town, the threat of the fire, and the response of state and federal agencies to the fire, as well as the response of local groups. The survey gave us the preliminary data we needed to launch a fieldwork project.

In planning a strategy to investigate the impact of the mine fire on the town's social fabric, we concluded that long-term, firsthand involvement with the problem was essential. Kroll-Smith's prior experience with fieldwork made him the logical candidate to move into town and map the complex beliefs, relationships, and coping strategies that evolved over the next several months as Centralians sought to make sense out of their predicament. On March 7, 1983, Kroll-Smith moved into a house on the south end of town, less than a hundred yards from where a fire-related cave-in two years previously had almost swallowed a twelve-year-old boy. The two-story house was attached to a row of homes that had been built by a mining company fifty years earlier. In that house, Kroll-Smith lived and worked for eight months. A gas monitor in the basement assured at least that an alarm would signal the presence of dangerous gases. In the end, the only serious threat from gas was seepage from an improperly sealed natural gas stove.[3]

Even before the fieldwork phase began, we realized that our techniques of data gathering and the nature of some of the information we sought would be perceived by diverse groups within the community as having immediate relevance for them in reacting to the problem. If we tried to explain to any group that we could not release our findings to them, but that eventually we would publish insights into the roots of their misery, we risked being excluded from group activities. Entrance into Centralia and its trust depended on cooperating with these struggling groups. In short, we knew that as we were interpreting Centralians, they would be interpreting us and our data, ensuring a place for sociology in their struggle to reach a consensus on the destiny of their town. Gouldner was probably thinking of collective turmoil when he observed, "knowing and changing are distinguishable but not separate processes."[4]

Our expectations that factions in town would solicit our perceptions of their situation forced us to deal with a complex moral and methodological quandary. The interests of science and social action are frequently argued to be in competition. To abandon one's scientific detachment while working with a collective in crisis is to place the scientific value of the research at risk. Yet one maintains the scientific posture at the risk of lending tacit support to the continuance of a "bad" situation. In considering Centralia's trauma and our simultaneous responsibilities to the community and to science, the distinction between social science and advocacy appeared to us particularly forced and artificial.

It was apparent to us that our involvement with Centralia was itself a topic for inquiry, and we needed to strengthen our capacity to reflect critically on that involvement. The questions we faced were two: How were we to reinforce our interpretation of ourselves interpreting Centralia? By what moral guideline would we release information to the community?

The first question was comparatively easy to answer. Couch assumed the role of the silent partner, concerned but not involved with the minutiae of daily life in Centralia. His role in the community was limited to organizing the survey, examining government and historical materials, attending a limited number of community events, and reflecting on the influence our research was having on the flow of events. Couch's position of limited liability proved indispensable in achieving that measure of detachment necessary to interpret critically our roles in the Centralia drama.

The question about what ethical standard to follow in releasing information to the community proved more difficult to answer. We agreed after much discussion that data would be released only when we both concurred that it would further the efforts of residents to achieve a common interpretation of their predicament and to heal the divisions within the community.

In adopting this moral guideline for the release of information, we expected some groups to perceive us as being nonsupportive of their immediate goals, strategies, or tactics. In Centralia, being perceived as nonsupportive was tantamount to being an enemy. For example, we were denied access to the inner circles of two groups because we had withheld from them some portions of our data. However, we recognized that all groups in Centralia held in common the objective of community unity, albeit on their own terms. In the case, then, of those groups we could not support, we decided to represent their needs to those groups with whom we established a working relationship. In short, we took the stated objective of all the groups—to rally the town around a common understanding of its crisis and its destiny—as a moral goal worthy of our support.

Our experiences in Centralia convinced us that to research a community in crisis carries with it a moral obligation to further the developmental needs of the community. It is also our belief that a commitment to enhance the problem-solving skills of a community need not conflict with the commitment that sociologists make to their colleagues and students. When we study a group or community, particularly one in profound crisis, we represent both researchers and moral agents. As moral agents, we become part of the problem and the solution—and part of our own data.

For those sociologists who share our ethical position, and who seek to do research in communities while simultaneously working toward the betterment of those communities, we offer the following tentative guidelines:

(1) Suggest options but do not choose for the community. Support those of its choices that promise to heal and not divide.

(2) Do not expect to establish rapport with all competing groups. Respond empathetically to expressions of hostility and anger on the part of those groups whose strategies you cannot support.

(3) If feasible, when group tactics preclude your support, be prepared to represent the group's needs to those with whom you are working more closely.

(4) In responding to requests for information and guidance you cannot provide, be forthcoming in admitting your limitations. But, do not underestimate the insights sociology can provide.

(5) If you are fortunate enough to have a collaborator, carefully consider the division of labor in light of the goals of the research and the needs of the community.

Notes

Introduction: A Dying Coal Town

1. Stephen R. Couch and J. Stephen Kroll-Smith, "The Chronic Technical Disaster: Towards a Social Scientific Perspective," *Social Science Quarterly*, 66 (1985):564-75.

1. King Coal Built a Town but Not a Community

1. In a similar vein, a community sociologist notes that in emergent nations the " 'rediscovery' of a past previously dormant, ambiguous or non-existent" is common practice. Joseph R. Gusfield, *Community, A Critical Response* (New York: Harper and Row, 1975) 38.

2. Ben J. Wattenberg, ed. *The Statistical History of the United States* (New York: Basic Books, 1976), 590, 592.

3. John K. Mumford, *Anthracite* (New York: Industries Publishing Co., 1925), 81.

4. Clifton K. Yearley, Jr., *Enterprise In Anthracite* (Baltimore: Johns Hopkins University Press, 1961), 30-31, 83-84.

5. Robert F. Archer, *The History of the Lehigh Valley Railroad* (Berkeley: Hawell North, 1977), 75.

6. Rowland Bertoff, "The Social Order of the Anthracite Region, 1825-1902," *The Pennsylvania Magazine of History and Biography* (July 1965), 262.

7. Harold W. Aurand, *From the Molly Maguires to the United Mine Workers: The Social Ecology of an Industrial Union, 1869-1897* (Philadelphia: Temple University Press 1971), 20.

8. J.H. Beers, *Historical and Biographical Annals of Columbia and Montour Counties, Pennsylvania*, vol. 1 (Chicago: J.H. Beers) 202; J.H. Battle, ed., *History of Columbia and Montour Counties, Pennsylvania* (Chicago: A. Warner, 1887), 312; Centenary Committee, *St. Ignatius Church Centenary, 1869-1969* (Centralia, 1969),

5; Ira F. Roadarmel, *Centralia Centennial, 1866-1966* (Centralia, 1966), 4.

9. John E. Geschwindt, State Library of Pennsylvania, letter to authors, March 27, 1984.

10. Battle, *History of Columbia*, 311.

11. Battle, *History of Columbia*, 313-316; Beers, *Annals of Columbia*, 204-206; Centenary Committee, *St. Ignatius Church*, 19-21.

12. Roadarmel, *Centralia Centennial*, 7-8

13. Aurand, *Molly Maguires*, 23, 24.

14. Yearley, *Enterprise In Anthracite*, 206-207.

15. Aurand, *Molly Maguires*, 25. See also Wayne G. Broehl, Jr., *The Molly Maguires* (Cambridge: Harvard University Press, 1964) 295-96. Broehl's is the most balanced account of the Mollies published to date. Whether seen as Irish freedom fighters or terrorists, the Mollies took part in the violence and conflict of the anthracite region during Centralia's early years.

16. Centenary Committee, *St. Ignatius Church*, 16; Battle, *History of Columbia*, 314.

17. Beers, *Annals of Columbia*, 205; Roadarmel, *Centralia Centennial*, 8. In 1875, "a crowd of striking miners marched on the colliery and drove away the workmen and burned the breaker to the ground" in protest over the hiring of "blacklegs," or scab laborers (Centenary Committee, *St. Ignatius Church*, 13).

18. Battle, *History of Columbia*, 314; Beers, Annals of Columbia, 203; Craig A. Newton, "Centralia: Tempered by Coal and Fire," unpublished paper (1976).

19. Adolf W. Schalek and D.C. Henning, eds., *History of Schuylkill County, Pa.*, vol. 1 (Harrisburg: State Historical Society, 1907) 158.

20. *History of Schuylkill County* (New York: W.W. Munsell, 1881) 53-54; Aurand, *Molly Maguires*, 66.

21. Howard N. Eavenson, *The First Century and a Quarter of the American Coal Industry* (Baltimore: Waverly Press, 1942), 378.

22. Aurand, *Molly Maguires*, 72, 80-81, 91-92, 106, 110-14, 129-30, 138-42.

23. For an account of a local strike in 1896 that illustrates the weakness of Centralia's internal political structure, see Barbara Knox

Homrighaus, Stephen R. Couch, and J. Stephen Kroll-Smith, "Building a Town but Preventing a Community: A Social History of Centralia, Pennsylvania," in Lance E. Metz, ed., *Proceedings of the Canal History and Technology Symposium* (Easton, Pa.: Center for Canal History and Technology, 1985) 69-91.

24. Stephen R. Couch, "The Coal and Iron Police in Anthracite Country," in David L. Salay, ed., *Hard Coal, Hard Times: Ethnicity and Labor in the Anthracite Region* (Scranton, Pa.: Anthracite Museum Press, 1984) 100-119; Jeremiah Patrick Shalloo, *Private Police: With Special Reference to Pennsylvania* (Philadelphia: American Academy of Political and Social Sciences, 1933).

25. For classic descriptions of deviance and group boundaries, see Emile Durkheim, *The Division of Labor in Society* (New York: The Free Press, 1984) 62-63; Kai Erikson, *The Wayward Puritans* (New York: Macmillan, 1984).

26. Aurand, *Molly Maguires*, 21.

27. On the concept of internal colonialism, see Michael Hechter, *Internal Colonialism: The Celtic Fringe in British National Development, 1536-1966* (Berkeley: University of California Press, 1975); Pablo Gonzales-Casanova, "Internal Colonialism and National Development," *Studies in Comparative International Development,* 1965, no. 1: 27-37; and Paul Nyden, "An Internal Colony: Labor Conflict and Capitalism in Appalachian Coal," *Insurgent Sociologist,* 1979, no. 8: 33-43. In essence, the concept draws an analogy between the uneven and exploitative development of regions within a country and the similar treatment of one country by another, or colonialism.

28. E. Digby Baltzell, *Philadelphia Gentlemen: The Making of a National Upper Class* (Glencoe, Ill.: Free Press, 1958) 118.

29. Battle, *History of Columbia,* 312-16; Geschwindt, letter; Beers, *Annals of Columbia,* 204.

30. Deed 260, Deed Book 85, June 27, 1912, Bloomsburg, Pa., Columbia County Courthouse, 286-87.

31. Geschwindt, letter.

32. Bertoff, *Social Order of Anthracite Region,* 263.

33. John E. Bodnar, "Family and Community in Pennsylvania's Anthracite Region, 1900-1940," *Pennsylvania Heritage* 9 (Summer 1983): 13-17.

34. Anthony F.C. Wallace, "The Miners of St. Clair: Family Class, and Ethnicity in a Mining Town in Schuylkill County, 1850-1880," in David L. Salay, ed., *Hard Coal, Hard Times: Ethnicity and Labor in the Anthracite Region* (Scranton, Pa.: Anthracite Museum Press, 1984) 1-16.

35. Ibid., 7.

36. Beers, *Annals of Columbia*, 206; Centenary Committee, *St. Ignatius Church*, 32.

37. William Gudelunas and Stephen R. Couch, "Would a Protestant or Polish Kennedy Have Won? A Local Test of Ethnicity and Religion in the Presidential Election of 1960," *Ethnic Groups* 3 (December 1980), 1-21.

38. Wallace, *Miners of St. Clair*, 11. See also Anthony F.C. Wallace, *St. Clair* (New York: Alfred A. Knopf, 1987).

39. Battle, *History of Columbia*, 317; Roadarmel, *Centralia Centennial*, 10; Newton, "Tempered by Coal and Fire".

40. Bertoff, *Social Order of Anthracite Region*, 284-85.

41. David L. Salay, "Editor's Introduction," *Hard Coal, Hard Times*, x-xi.

42. Centenary Committee, *St. Ignatius Church*, 13, 18.

43. William A. Gudelunas, "The Ethno-Religious Factor Reaches Fruition: The Politics of Hard Coal, 1945-1972," in Salay, *Hard Coal, Hard Times*, 171.

44. U.S. Bureau of the Census, *Statistical Abstract of the United States, 1977*, 98th ed. (Washington, D.C.: Government Printing Office) 751.

45. Gudelunas, "Ethno-Religious Factor," 171.

46. Geschwindt, letter.

47. *Pottsville Republican*, 12/4/08.

48. *Bloomsburg Democratic Sentinel*, 12/4/08; *Pottsville Republican*, 12/4/08.

49. *Bloomsburg Democratic Sentinel*, 12/14/08, 1/8/09.

50. Ibid., 1/8/09.

51. Ibid., 12/8/08; 12/29/08.

52. Ibid., 12/29/08.

53. Ibid.

54. Ibid., 1/8/09.

55. Ibid., 3/2/09, 3/30/09.

2. The Engineering Puzzle, 1962-1981

1. Roger E. Kasperson and K. David Pijawka, "Societal Response to Hazards and Major Hazard Events: Comparing Natural and Technological Hazards," *Public Administration Review* 45 (1985): 12, 14. The difficulty that local communities face in mobilizing to cope with the chronic technological disaster and their dependence on sources of power remote from the affected populations are illustrated in a fine study of the Love Canal toxic waste disaster: Adeline G. Levine, *Love Canal: Science, Politics and People* (Lexington, Mass.: Lexington Books, 1982).

2. Robbins and Associates, *Centralia Mine Fire Abatement Alternatives*, December 12, 1980, 37-38.

3. Ibid., 38; *Shamokin News-Item*, 8/22/62.

4. Robbins and Associates, *Abatement Alternatives*, 38.

5. Ibid.

6. Ibid., 38-39.

7. Ibid., 39.

8. Ibid.

9. *Shamokin News-Item*, 9/7/66.

10. Robbins and Associates, *Abatement Alternatives*, 39-40.

11. *Shamokin News-Item*, 5/23/69.

12. Robbins and Associates, Abatement Alternatives, 40.

13. *Shamokin News-Item*, 5/23/69.

14. *Shamokin News-Item*, 5/27/69.

15. Robbins and Associates, *Abatement Alternatives*, 40.

16. *Shamokin News-Item*, 6/16/69.

17. Ibid.

18. Robbins and Associates, *Abatement Alternatives*, 40.

19. Ibid.

20. Ibid., 41.

21. *Shamokin News-Item*, 12/8/76.

22. *Shamokin News-Item*, 1/25/78.

23. Ibid.; Robbins and Associates, *Abatement Alternatives*, 42.

24. *Shamokin News-Item*, 12/8/76.

25. Robbins and Associates, *Abatement Alternatives*, 42-43.

26. Ibid., 44.

27. Charles A. Beasley, memo to Walter N. Heine, 6/27/79.

28. *Shamokin News-Item*, 8/8/79.

29. *Shamokin News-Item*, 12/4/79.

30. GAI Consultants, Inc., *Engineering Analysis and Evaluation of the Centralia Mine Fire*, 2 vols., June 1983.

31. *Shamokin News-Item*, 12/8/79.

32. Robbins and Associates, *Abatement Alternatives*, 44.

33. Office of Surface Mining and Reclamation, U.S. Department of the Interior, "Relocation Plan: Centralia Mine Fire Reclamation Project," 1980.

34. *Shamokin News-Item*, 2/25/80; 4/8/80; 6/27/80.

35. Charles A. Beasley, memo to Assistant Regional Director, AML, Region 1, and Budget Officer, Region 1, 4/30/80.

36. Helen Richards, memo to Charles A. Beasley and Wesley R. Booker, 5/5/80.

37. Patrick B. Boggs, memo to Walter N. Heine, 11/5/80.

38. John R. Woodrum, memo to Marion Turzai, 10/31/80.

39. Boggs, memo to Heine.

40. Office of Surface Mining (1980) Position Paper.

41. C.H. McConnell, letter to Walter Heine, 6/16/80.

42. *Shamokin News-Item*, 7/8/80; 12/4/79.

43. Earl R. Cunningham, memo to Charles A. Beasley, 1980.

44. Helen Richards, memo to Beasley.

45. Bureau of Mines, U.S. Department of the Interior, *Problems in Control of the Centralia Mine Fire* (Washington, D.C.,: U.S. Government Printing Office, 1980).

46. *Shamokin News-Item*, 9/8/80; 9/30/80.

47 *Shamokin News-Item*, 12/9/80.

48. Robert P. Gephart, Jr., "Making Sense of Organizationally Based Environmental Disasters," *Journal of Management*, 1984, no. 10: 206.

49. Kurt Lang and Gladys Engel Lang, "Collective Responses to the Threat of Disaster," in George H. Grosser et al., eds., *The Threat of Impending Disaster* (Cambridge: MIT Press, 1964) 67; Andrew Baum, Jerome E. Singer, and Carlene S. Baum, "Stress and Environment," *Journal of Social Issues* 37 (1981):25-26.

50. K. Lang and G.E. Lang, "Collective Responses to Threat," 71. An interesting hypothesis links sustained threat of the unknown stemming from environmental hazards to hysterical contagion. See

Steven P. Schwartz, Paul E. White, and Robert G. Hughes, "Environmental Threats, Communities, and Hysteria," *Journal of Public Health* 6 (1985): 58-75.

3. Ambiguous Evidence and Contradictory Signals

1. The most recent reviews of the literature on the social response to immediate-impact disaster are E. L. Quarantelli and Russell R. Dynes, "Response to Social Crisis and Disaster," *Annual Review of Sociology* 3 (1977): 23-49; Jerry D. Rose, *Outbreaks: The Sociology of Collective Behavior* (New York: Free Press, 1981), Chap 2; Gary A. Kreps, "Sociological Inquiry and Disaster Research," *Annual Review of Sociology* 10 (1984): 309-330. For one of the few ethnographic accounts of a community response to a natural disaster, see James B. Taylor Louis A. Zurcher and William H. Key, *Tornado: A Community Responds to Disaster* (Seattle, Wash.: University of Washington Press, 1970). For a conceptual account of the emergence of the therapeutic or altruistic community see, Ralph H. Turner, "Types of Solidarity in the Reconstituting of Groups," *Pacific Sociological Review* 19(1976): 60-68; Allen Barton, *Communities in Disaster* (New York: Doubleday, 1969), Chap. 5, "The Altruistic Community"; Thomas R. Forrest, "Needs and Group Emergence," *American Behavioral Scientist* 16 (1973): 413-425.

2. Recent support for the idea that community response to chronic technological disasters is more likely to be divisive than therapeutic or altruistic comes from several sources. In their report to the Federal Emergency Management Agency on the interpretations by Love Canal residents of the toxic chemicals plaguing their neighborhoods, Fowlkes and Miller discovered several conflicting definitions of the scope and seriousness of the problem. See Martha R. Fowlkes and Patricia Y. Miller, *Love Canal: The Social Construction of Disaster*, Federal Emergency Management Agency Work Unit no. 6441E, 1982. An ongoing study of the asbestos contamination of a portion of Globe, Arizona, reveals serious discord among residents who have varying interpretations of the amount of risk involved and of what, if anything, should be done to mitigate it. See Kasperson and Pijawka, "Societal Response to Hazards," 7-18. Gephart found controversy surrounding the Santa Barbara, Califor-

nia, oil spill. (Gephart "Making Sense of Organizationally Based Environmental Disasters," 205-25). The issue is not simply intra-community conflict; as Fowlkes and Miller, Kasperson and Pijawka, and Gephart point out, it is also conflict between the community and those government agencies and legislators responsible for responding to the crisis.

3. Recent work on reality disjunctures informs the conceptual basis for the following discussion. See Melvin Pollner, "The Very Coinage of Your Brain: The Anatomy of Reality Dis-junctures," *Philosophy of the Social Sciences* 5 (1975): 411-30; Jeff Coulter, "Perceptual Accounts and Interpretive Asymmetries," *Sociology* 9 (1975): 385-96; Peter Eglin, "Resolving Reality Disjunctures on Telegraph Avenue: A Study of Practical Reasoning," *Canadian Journal of Sociology* 4 (1979): 359-77.

4. *Shamokin News-Item*, 3/30/80.

5. Pennsylvania Department of Health, Division of Environmental Health, "Centralia Health Hazards," July 1983 (mimeograph). To give the reader some idea of the effects of long-term exposure to these gases, the following are symptoms of chronic exposure: carbon monoxide—lassitude, headaches, dizziness; sulfur dioxide—respiratory disease; carbon dioxide—shortness of breath, headaches.

6. Bureau of Mines, *Problems in Control of Centralia Fire*.

7. *Shamokin News-Item*, 3/30/80.

8. For a discussion of the ambiguous role of social service organizations in communities in conflict, as well as advice to communities for making use of such services, see J. Stephen Kroll-Smith and Samuel Garula, "The Real Disaster Is Above Ground: Community Conflict and Grassroots Organization in Centralia," *Small Town*, January–February 1985, 7-12.

9. The core of Simmel's and Coser's reasoning is the positive effects of conflict for groups and organizations. See George Simmel, *Conflict and the Web of Group Affiliations* (New York: Free Press, 1955) 14-16; Lewis A. Coser, *The Functions of Social Conflict* (New York: Free Press, 1956) Chap. 5.

10. James Coleman, "Community Disorganization," in Robert Merton and James A. Nisbet, eds., *Social Problems*, 1st ed. (New York: Harcourt, Brace and World, 1966) 673.

4. A Group Emerges and the Town Divides

 1. *Philadelphia Inquirer*, 12/6/81.
 2. *Shamokin News-Item*, 2/16/81.
 3. Studies of environmental stress suggest that when people feel
threatened by what they perceive as an uncontrollable and unpre-
dictable ecological hazard, they will search urgently for a viable
adaptive strategy. For several discussions on human response to
perceived uncontrollable situations, see Gary W. Evans, issue editor
"Environmental Stress," *Journal of Social Issues* 37 (1981). See also
K. Lang and G.E. Lang, "Collective Responses to Threat," 58-75.
 4. For a thorough discussion of the sociological dimensions of
belief, see James T. Borhek and Richard F. Curtis, *A Sociology of
Belief* (New York: John Wiley and Sons, 1975). A classic statement
of the social foundations of belief is found in Talcott Parsons, *The
Social System* (New York: Macmillan, 1951), Chap. 8.
 5. We offer an extended discussion of threat belief systems and
collective action in J. Stephen Kroll-Smith and Stephen R. Couch,
"The Chronic Technical Disaster, Small Town Conflict and the Social Construction of Threat Beliefs," in Edward J. Miller and Robert
P. Wolensky, eds., *The Small City and Regional Community* (Stevens
Point, Wisc.: Foundation Press, 1984) 262-70. Mileti et al. note that
the concept of risk perception "has not been particularly fruitful as
a predictor of . . . socially important behaviors, e.g., adoption or
not of lifesaving adjustments. It appears that hazard perception studies are not likely to get very far until the social constraints within
which the perception-behavior links occurring are explicitly incorporated into theory and research design." Dennis Mileti et al.,
Human Systems in Extreme Environments: A Sociological Perspective,
Monograph no. 21 (Boulder, Colo.: Institute of Behavioral Science
1975), 33-34. Treating hazard perception from the perspective of
the sociology of belief is one means by which to advance our understanding of the links between the interpretations of danger and
accompanying behaviors.
 6. This is quite different from what happens in natural disasters.
For example, Rayner found that "an element which seems to influence people's behavior during threat of crisis is the commonly found
myth that 'it can't happen to me.' This legend often seems to serve
the function of minimizing danger." Jeanette F. Rayner, *Hurricane*

Barbara: A Study of the Evacuation of Ocean City (Washington, D.C.: National Academy of Sciences, 1953) 17-18. For residents living on the south side of Centralia, danger appeared too real and imminent to be reduced to a minimalist interpretation.

7. Perhaps identifying with the worst-case scenarios functions to ward off the anxiety of being overwhelmed by the unforseen. See Martha Wolfenstein, *Disaster: A Psychological Essay* (Glencoe Ill.: Free Press, 1957) Chap. 1.

8. *Shamokin News-Item*, 3/13/81.

9. All of the above witnesses in the Mines and Energy hearings were relocated within several months of their testimonies.

10. Centralia itself does not have a newspaper. But most Centralians rely on the *Shamokin News-Item* for their local news. Shamokin, a city of about 25,000 inhabitants, is located approximately ten miles west of Centralia.

11. *Shamokin News-Items*, 6/20/81.

12. Ibid. 12/12/79.

13. In his treatment of the media and natural disasters, Wenger notes, "The content and reporting of the mass media present a distorted, mythical, perhaps inaccurate, depiction of actual disaster behavior." Dennis Wenger, "Mass Media and Disasters," Preliminary Paper no. 98 (Newark: University of Delaware, Disaster Research Center) 9. In a study of two newspapers, Combs and Slovic report a marked tendency to overestimate and emphasize hazards associated with homocides, accidents, and disasters. See Barbara Combs and Paul Slovic, "Newspaper Coverage of Causes of Death" *Journalism Quarterly*, 56(1979):837-49. If it is true that the media have difficulty in rendering unbiased, realistic accounts of natural disasters, then we can expect that they will have an even more difficult time reporting accurately the ill-defined, difficult to detect, and almost impossible to predict chronic technological disaster. Problems in media coverage of a chronic technological disaster were addressed by Schwartz, White, and Hughes, "Environmental Threats, Communities, and Hysteria," 58-77.

14. *Shamokin News-Item*, 4/2/81; 4/4/81.

15. Ibid., 3/30/81.

16. Fowlkes and Miller note that at Love Canal, residents believed that the only agencies they could trust were those having "nothing tangibly at stake in the present and future of the com-

munity." The media were perceived as being more trustworthy than state and federal agencies. See Fowlkes and Miller, "Love Canal: Social Construction," 119.

17. *Shamokin News-Item*, 1/7/81, 3/16/81, 4/28/81.

18. Ibid., 3/21/81.

19. Ibid.

20. Ibid., 11/4/81.

21. In a book, the reporter clearly expressed his identification with the CC and his firm conviction that both he and the group were persecuted. The book reads as a personal attack on those government officials and ordinary citizens of Centralia who disagreed with the CC's position. The book parallels the newspaper's coverage in that it reduces a complex crisis to conspiracy theories and maladjusted personalities. David DeKok, *Unseen Danger* (Philadelphia: University of Pennsylvania Press, 1987).

22. Stephen Phelps, "Centralia 1981: A Report on the Positions and Interests of Parties Involved in Responses to the Mine Fire" (Rochester, N.Y.: Institute on Man and Science, 1981).

23. Baum et al. suggest that the psychic costs of overestimating risk may result in states of anxious suffering as people wait for anticipated "physical events that never come to pass." A. Baum, J.E. Singer, and C.S. Baum, "Stress and the Environment," 4-35.

24. Ibid. Baum et al. refer to two kinds of coping styles: emotional coping, in which an individual attempts to adjust to stressors by consciously controlling feelings of fear or dread, and instrumental coping, which attempts to do something to alleviate the external problem itself. A third kind of response—what we call confrontational coping—can be seen as having occurred in Centralia. In this style, coping serves as a manifest instrumental function in demanding that something be done about the problem, and also serves latent emotional functions in allowing the venting of frustrations through confrontation.

5. Confrontation and Conflict

1. Coser has referred to this type of emotive conflict occasioned by the "need for tension release" as "nonrealistic conflict." It is nonrealistic conflict to the extent that the goal of problem solving

or instrumental change becomes subordinate to emotive display. Coser, *Functions of Social Conflict*, 42-55.

2. *Shamokin News-Item*, 4/23/81.

3. Social "hatred is directed against the member of a group, not from personal motives, but because the member represents a danger to the preservation of the group." George Simmel, *Conflict and the Web of Group Affiliations* (New York: Free Press, 1955), 43-44.

4. *Shamokin News-Item*, 3/19/81.

5. Ibid, 3/30/81.

6. Ibid, 4/25/81.

7. Ibid, 6/23/81.

8. Ibid, 7/29/81.

9. Ibid, 7/21/81. Ironically, in the third and final buyout, which would begin in three years, many homeowners would receive several thousand dollars more than the market value of their homes. In spite of its own attorney's advice, however, the OSM did not retreat. Twenty-seven families left the town, victims of a fire they did not start and a meanness of government spirit they could not comprehend.

10. A letter is composed for another without the hindrance of the presence of that other. Letter writing is an occasion for solidifying ideas and beliefs unencumbered by the presence of the audience, who might interrupt, question, or simply not attend to what is being said. Without the risk of a refractory audience, letter writing, like a soliloquy, encourages the self-affirmation that comes from unchallenged revelation. Neighbors contested and challenged the CC's interpretations of the fire. Letters, composed in isolation or among fellow CC members, provided an important context for the uncontested expression of the group's beliefs. In like manner, a letter received can be mulled over by the recipient, debated, and perhaps interpreted in a manner foreign to what the author had intended.

11. CC, letter to Richard Thornburgh, 4/26/81.

12. CC, letter to Ronald Reagan, 4/28/81.

13. CC, letter to James Watt, 8/25/81.

14. James Nelligan, letter to the CC, 5/1/81.

15. Robert Belfanti, letter to the CC, 8/12/81. The report in question, or some version of it, was subsequently released and proved to be of very little help.

16. Deputy Director Kenahan, letter from Bureau of Mines to the CC, 3/19/82.

17. Alan Ertel, letter to the CC, 2/22/82.

18. Robert Belfanti, letter to the CC, 3/2/82.

19. Governor's Deputy General Counsel, letter to the CC, 1/22/82.

20. Assistant Director of Abandoned Mine Lands, DOI, letter to the CC, 8/11/81.

21. Only about one-half of the correspondence was saved.

22. Robert Wolensky, "Municipal Government's Problem With Natural Disaster: A Structured Examination," unpublished paper.

23. Borough Council, minutes, 5/5/80.

24. Ibid., 3/3/80.

25. *Shamokin News-Item,* 5/18/81.

26. Borough Council Minutes, 5/2/81.

27. *Shamokin News-Item,* 5/18/81.

28. Concerned Citizens Minutes: 4/14/81.

29. The RAW and Nader's group had worked together in the past. It is possible that Nader representatives contacted the RAW and encouraged them to call.

30. Rural American Women, "Why We Are Involved In Centralia."

31. Director, Appalachia-Science in the Public Interest, letter to the CC, 11/11/82.

32. Executive Director, Delaware Valley Citizens' Council for Clean Air, letter to the CC, 11/8/82.

33. RAW news release, 10/9/81.

34. *Shamokin News-Item,* 10/6/81.

35. Ibid., 11/25/81.

36. It is interesting to note that several days after Watt's faux pas, the BOM issued a "gag order" for its Pennsylvania agency personnel, to "minimize the confusion that comes from multiple answers" (*Shamokin News-Item,* 12/2/81). In a direct reference to Watt, one regional representative commented, "Why gag us? We're not getting the headlines."

37. *Shamokin News-Item,* 11/24/81.

38. Annual Report, Catholic Social Services, Diocese of Harrisburg, Pennsylvania, 1985:3.

39. We can appreciate the significance of these trips if we con-

sider their meaning in relation to the concepts of center and periphery. Edward Shils, *Center and Periphery* (University of Chicago Press, 1975). Both Washington and Harrisburg are centers of political decision-making. Centralia is quite obviously located at the outer periphery of these centers, remote from the loci of power. Not unlike pilgrims who find themselves empowered by their journeys to sacred regions, the resolve of CC members strengthened through their contact with these centers of power. Moreover, similar to the bonding that occurs through the common experience of the pilgrimage, those who traveled to Washington and Harrisburg affirmed their commitment to one another and the plight of the group. Victor Turner and Edith Turner, *Image and Pilgrimage in Christian Culture* (New York: Columbia University Press, 1978).

40. Borough Council, minutes, 1/11/82.

41. Ibid., 3/8/82.

42. Ibid., 2/1/82.

43. Ibid., 4/26/82.

44. In the eyes of Centralians, the Campaign for Human Development was associated with the Irish Catholic Church.

45. *Shamokin News-Item*, 9/8/82.

46. Concerned Citizens, minutes, 9/28/82.

47. As one set of researchers reported: "We know a good deal about the strategies for crisis intervention that are most effective in helping individuals and communities deal with natural disasters. Much less is known through experience about what kinds of intervention strategies are most helpful when disasters are wrought by people." Jodie Kliman et al., "Natural and Human Made Disasters: Some Therapeutic and Epidemiological Implications for Crisis Intervention," in *Therapeutic Intervention*, ed. V. Rueveni, Ross U. Speck, and Joan L. Speck (New York: Human Science Press, 1982). Moreover, the dependence of the CC on this vertical-structure agency ensured that whatever difficulties the agency experienced would become difficulties for the group.

48. *Shamokin News-Item*, 9/14/82.

6. A Thwarted Struggle for Unity

1. *Shamokin News-Item*, 10/4/82, 10/5/82.

2. Ibid., 1/28/82 (Associated Press release).

3. Centralia Committee on Human Development, minutes, 12/7/82.

4. Ibid., 12/14/82.

5. Ibid.

6. Ibid., 12/17/82.

7. Ibid., 12/20/82.

8. For a discussion of "model of" and "model for" collective activities, see Clifford Geertz, *The Interpretation of Culture* (New York: Basic Books, 1973).

9. Centralia Committee on Human Development, "Quarterly Report to the Campaign for Human Development," January 1983.

10. The CCHD is similar to what has been called a "coordinating group." See Robert A. Stallings and E.L. Quarantelli, "Emergent Citizen Groups and Emergency Management," *Public Administration Review*, 45(1985):93-100.

11. Centralia Committee for Human Development, minutes, 3/7/83.

12. "Attribution processes are to be understood not only as a means of providing the individual with a veridical view of his world, but as a means of encouraging and maintaining his effective exercise of control in that world." H.H. Kelley, *Attribution in Social Interaction* (Morristown, N.J.: General Learning Corporation, 1971) 22. See also Ronnie Janoff Bulman and Camille B. Wortman, "Attributions of Blame and Coping in the 'Real World': Severe Victims React to Their Lot," *Journal of Personality and Social Psychology*, 35(1977):351-63.

13. *Shamokin News-Item*, 1/7/83.

14. Ibid., 10/7/83.

15. Copies of these speeches were obtained by the authors.

7. One Town, Many Groups

1. Office of Surface Mining, U.S. Bureau of Mines, "Centralia Mine Fire Assessment Drilling and Diagnostic Monitoring: Interim Report March 1983." "Mine temperatures were categorized into three zones: normal, an area which has standard . . . mine atmosphere, 55-65F; conditioned, an area which is being heated by mine gases, 100-200F; and a high temperature area which is presently burning, 400-1000F" (p. 3).

2. *Shamokin News-Item*: 4/25/83.

3. Ibid, 3/26/83.

4. Centralia Committee On Human Development, minutes, 3/22/83.

5. Centralia Committee On Human Development, minutes, 5/18/83.

6. "Citizens Proclamation," 5/26/83 (author unknown).

7. Borough Council, minutes, 5/26/83.

8. Ibid, 5/26/83.

9. Although, as we shall see, the organizing efforts of the CCHD met with considerable success after the public acknowledgment by the OSM that the fire was out of control and that a considerable portion of the community should be relocated. The fact that only when the material conditions of the fire were conclusively revealed was a measure of cooperative action possible is a point we will consider in chapter 8.

10. *Shamokin News-Item*, 6/2/83.

11. Ibid, 6/14/83.

12. Centralia Committee On Human Development, minutes, 6/8/83.

13. GAI Consultants, "Engineering Analysis," 11.

14. *Shamokin News-Item*, 7/13/83.

15. Borough Council, letter O the CCHD, 6/11/83.

16. CCHD, letter to Borough Council, 6/14/83.

17. "An Engineering Report to the Centralia Borough Council Assessing the OSM Report: 'Engineering Analysis and Evaluation of the Centralia Mine Fire,' " Taylor Associates, August 1983.

18. Robbins and Associates, April 1983.

19. "An Assessment of the Findings and Recommendations of the Report: 'Engineering Analysis and Evaluation of the Centralia Mine Fire' as prepared by: The Office of Surface Mining: August, 1983," Robbins and Associates, September 1983.

20. Kroll-Smith, then serving as a consultant to the CCHD, was asked by the Borough Council to sit on the committee, whose deliberations were to be private; any access we might have to its meetings would come through Kroll-Smith's participation. With that in mind, Kroll-Smith agreed to sit on the committee. This decision, however, led to a serious misunderstanding between the CCHD and the council.

21. *Shamokin News-Item*, 9/9/83.
22. Ibid, 9/11/83.
23. Borough Council, "Position Paper," 7/25/83.

8. "This Town Is Dead"

1. Department of Health, Commonwealth of Pennsylvania, "Health Related Problems Associated with Trenching and Excavating," August 1983.
2. *Shamokin News-Item*, 8/16/83.
3. Ibid, 9/10/83.
4. Ibid, 9/14/83.
5. Ibid, 9/23/83; 10/5/83.
6. Ibid, 9/23/83.
7. Residents to Save the Borough of Centralia, "Fact Sheet No. 2," September 17, 1983.

9. Making Sociological Sense of the Story

1. Regarding the critical psychological importance that communal attachments have for individuals, we need go no further than Durkheim's classic work on suicide: Emile Durkheim, *Suicide*, trans. George Simpson (1897; reprint, Glencoe, Ill.: Free Press, 1964). For a gripping study of a technological disaster that had severe social and psychological consequences, see Kai Erikson, *Everything in Its Path: Destruction of Community in the Buffalo Creek Flood* (New York: Simon and Schuster, 1976). That the destruction of the social community can itself be so severe as to cause death is illustrated in Colin Turnbull, *The Mountain People* (New York: Simon and Schuster, 1972).
2. Couch and Kroll-Smith, "The Chronic Technical Disaster," 564-75.
3. General Accounting Office, U.S. Congress, "Siting of Hazardous Waste Landfills and Their Correlation with Racial and Economic Status of Surrounding Communities," 1983.
4. Robert D. Bullard, "Solid Waste Sites and the Black Houston Community," *Sociological Inquiry* 53 (1983): 273-88. See also "Race Bias Found in Location of Toxic Waste Dumps," *New York Times*, April 16, 1987, A20.

5. The Love Canal area, located at the extreme northwestern corner of the city, is an incorporated part of the city. But the local government chose to ignore the Love Canal neighborhoods, throwing responsibility for the toxic waste predicament onto the shoulders of the fourteen hundred residents there. In other words, Love Canal was structurally similar to a small town. The local political response to the Love Canal disaster illustrates the vulnerability of those sections of cities determined by the political structure to be expendable.

6. A.F.C. Wallace, *Human Behavior in Extreme Situations: A Survey of the Literature and Suggestions for Further Research,* National Academy of Sciences–National Research Council, Washington, D.C., 1956.

7. For a brief review of the literature on extreme environments, see J. Eugene Hass and Thomas E. Drabek, "Community Disaster and System Stress: A Sociological Perspective," in Joseph E. McGrath, ed., *Social and Psychological Factors in Stress* (New York: Holt, Rinehart and Winston, 1970) 264-86.

8. Mileti et al., *Extreme Environments,* 1975.

9. For a discussion of the stages of the natural disaster, see Dwight W. Chapman, "A Brief Introduction to Contemporary Disaster Research," in George W. Baker and Dwight W. Chapman, eds., *Man and Society in Disaster* (New York: Basic Books, 1962) 3-22.

10. C. Wright Mills, *The Sociological Imagination* (New York: Oxford University Press, 1959).

11. Anthony F.C. Wallace, "Mazeway Disintegration: The Individual's Perception of Socio-Cultural Disorganization," *Human Organization* 16 (1957):25.

12. Ibid., 24.

13. Sigmund Freud, *The Future of an Illusion* (New York: Doubleday, 1927) 21.

14. Beverly Raphael, *When Disaster Strikes* (New York: Basic Books, 1986). "Most of the initial rescue work is done by those who are themselves victims of the disaster, long before formal assistance arrives." (p. 72).

15. Ibid., 68.

16. E.L. Quarantelli and Russell R. Dynes, "Community Conflict: Its Absence and Its Presence in Natural Disasters," *Mass Emergencies,* 1(1976):139-152.

17. Ralph H. Turner, "Types of Solidarity in the Reconstituting of Groups," *Pacific Sociological Review* 10 (1967): 62.

18. Ibid., 63.

19. Andrew Baum, Raymond Fleming, and Jerome E. Singer, "Coping with Victimization by Technological Disaster," *Journal of Social Issues* 39 (1983): 122.

20. K. Lang and G.E. Lang, "Collective Responses to the Threat," 58.

21. Barton, *Communities In Disaster*, 40.

22. Fowlkes and Miller, *Love Canal: Social Construction*, 98.

23. Roger E. Kasperson and K. David Pijawka, "Societal Response to Hazards and Major Hazard Events: Comparing Natural and Technological Hazards," *Public Administration Review* 45(1985):16.

24. Beverly H. Cuthbertson and Joanne M. Nigg, "Technological Disaster and the Nontherapeutic Community," *Environment and Behavior*, 19(1987):468.

25. Coser, *The Functions of Social Conflict*, 1956.

26. R. I. Kutak, "Sociology of Crises: The Louisville Flood of 1937," *Social Forces* 17 (1938):66-72.

27. Gary A. Kreps, "Research Needs and Policy Issues on Mass Media," in *Disasters and the Mass Media Workshop, February 1979*. Committee on Disasters and the Mass Media. Washington, D.C.: National Academy of Sciences, 1980: 35-74.

28. Kasperson and Pijawka, "Societal Response to Hazards," 7.

29. R.W. Kates, ed., *Managing Technological Hazards: Research Needs and Opportunities* (Boulder: University of Colorado Institute of Behavioral Science, 1977, 250); Clark University, *Project Summary: Improving the Societal Management of Technological Hazards*, Center for Technology, Environment and Development, 1979.

30. Levine, *Love Canal: Science, Politics and People*; Fowlkes and Miller, *Love Canal: Social Construction*; see also Rae Zimmerman, "The Relationship of Emergency Management to Government Policies on Man-Made Technological Disaster," *Public Administration Review* 45 (1985): 29-39.

31. Slovic et al., "Rating the Risks," 16.

32. Kasperson and Pijawka, "Societal Response to Hazards," p.14; Couch and Kroll-Smith, "Chronic Technical Disaster," 564-75.

33. Kliman et al., "Natural and Human-Made Disasters."

34. Ibid., 267.

Appendix: Participatory Research in Centralia

1. Herbert Gans, "Sociology In America: The Discipline and the Public," *American Sociological Review* 54 (1989):2.

2. William I. Torry, "Anthropology and Disaster Research," *Disasters* 3 (1979): 43.

3. Please note, however, that Kroll-Smith lived in town for only eight months. It is not clear what effects several years of exposure to low levels of toxic gases might have on the human organism.

4. Alvin W. Gouldner, *The Coming Crisis of Western Sociology* (New York: Basic Books, 1970).

Index

Appalachia, Northern, 1, 18-20
Appalachian Redevelopment
   Act, 31
Appalachian Regional Commis-
   sion, 32, 35

Bureau of Mines, 32, 33; disa-
   grees with OSM, 36; enters
   into agreement with OSM,
   37

Catholic Social Services, 101-
   02; arranges grant for CC,
   104-07
Center for Responsive Law, 94
Centralia: attachment structure
   in, 15; historical image of,
   13, 14; influence of Lehigh
   Valley Railroad in shaping,
   17, 18; origin of name, 17;
   physical description of, 1, 2;
   population fluctuations in,
   17, 20-21, 24; recurrent
   physical catastrophes in, 22-
   27
Centralia Borough Council, 90;
   conducts referendums, 92-
   94, 150; criticized by CC,
   103-04; experiences trouble
   organizing meetings, 147;
   hires independent engineer,
   144; structure of, 91
Centralia Committee on Human Development, 110-11,
   135; develops internal organization, 112-14; hires inde-

pendent engineer, 144;
   organizes neighborhood area
   meetings, 148-49; public
   meeting structure, 136, 137,
   138; refuses to adopt interpretation of fire, 114; sought
   to serve as model for conflict
   resolution, 115, 136
Centralia Homeowners Association, 149, 153, 154-56
Centralia Input Task Force,
   146
chronic technological disaster,
   4; causes intramural conflict,
   168-69, 184-85 n 2; characteristics of, 9, 163; chal-
   lenges posed by, 106, 182 n
   1; creates social instability,
   164; defined as engineering
   puzzle, 29; demands of overwhelm communities, 161; no
   legislative authority for managing, 38; source of symbolic
   activity, 166; stress on social
   system, 158
citizens proclamation, 140
Citizens to Save the Borough,
   119, 155
Citizens to Save Byrnesville,
   118-19
coal and iron police, 19
coal industry, 15, 18-20; demise of, 23-24; and Lehigh
   Valley Railroad, 16, 26-28;
   and Philadelphia and Read
   ing Railroad, 16

DATE DUE

WITHDRAWN